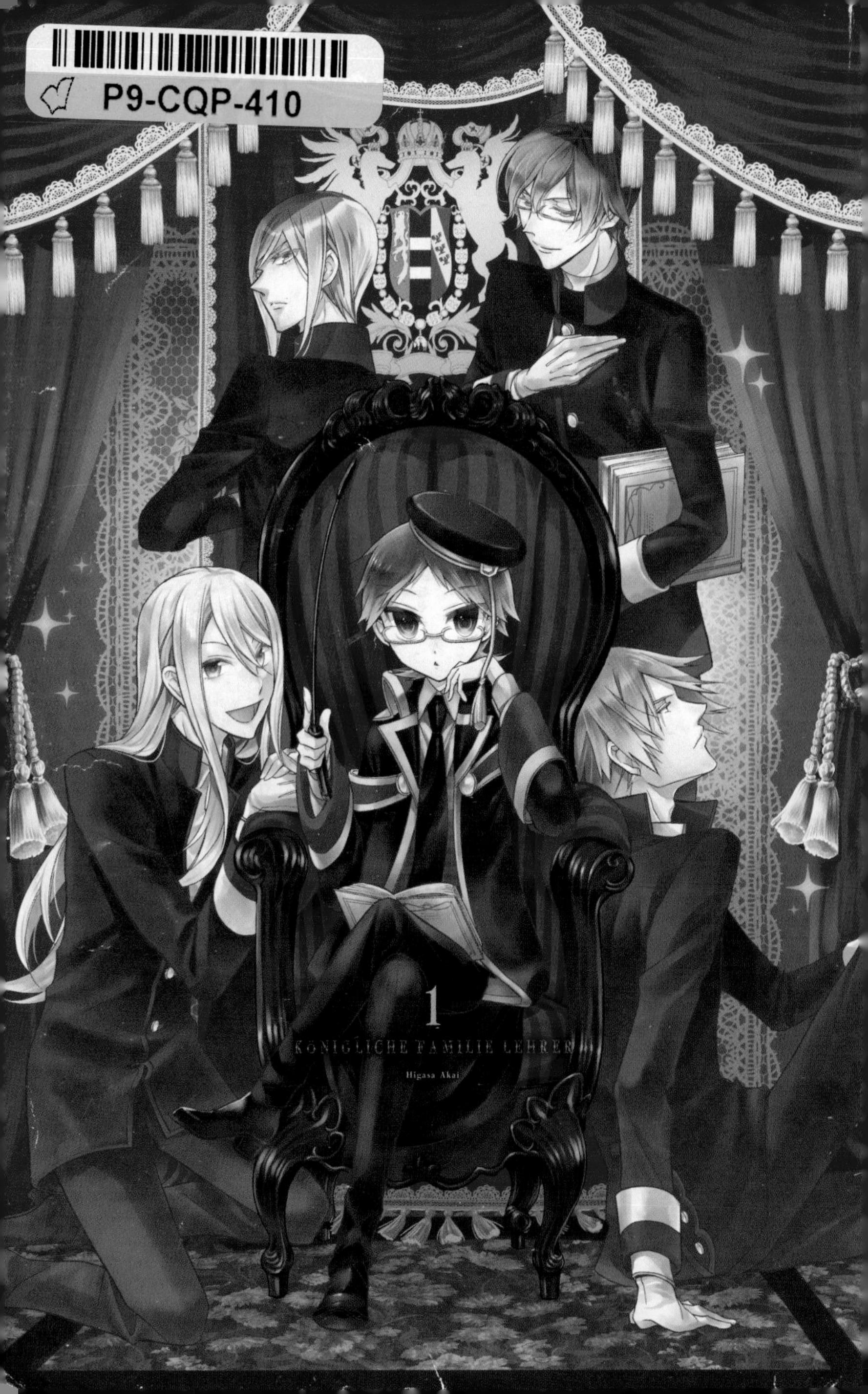
1
KÖNIGLICHE FAMILIE LEHRER
Higasa Akai

CONTENTS

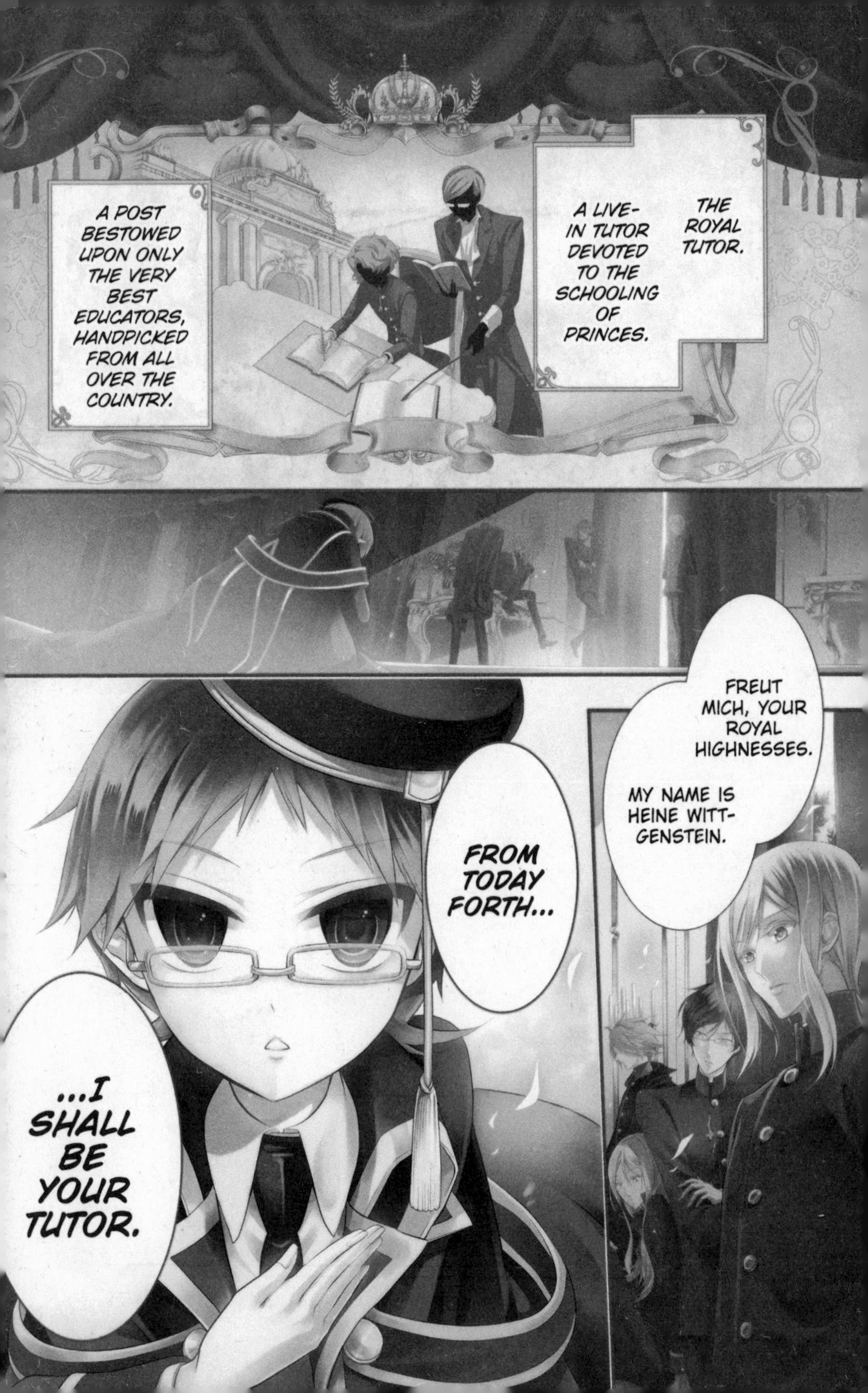
THE ROYAL TUTOR.
A LIVE-IN TUTOR DEVOTED TO THE SCHOOLING OF PRINCES.
A POST BESTOWED UPON ONLY THE VERY BEST EDUCATORS, HANDPICKED FROM ALL OVER THE COUNTRY.
FREUT MICH, YOUR ROYAL HIGHNESSES.
MY NAME IS HEINE WITT-GENSTEIN.
FROM TODAY FORTH...
...I SHALL BE YOUR TUTOR.

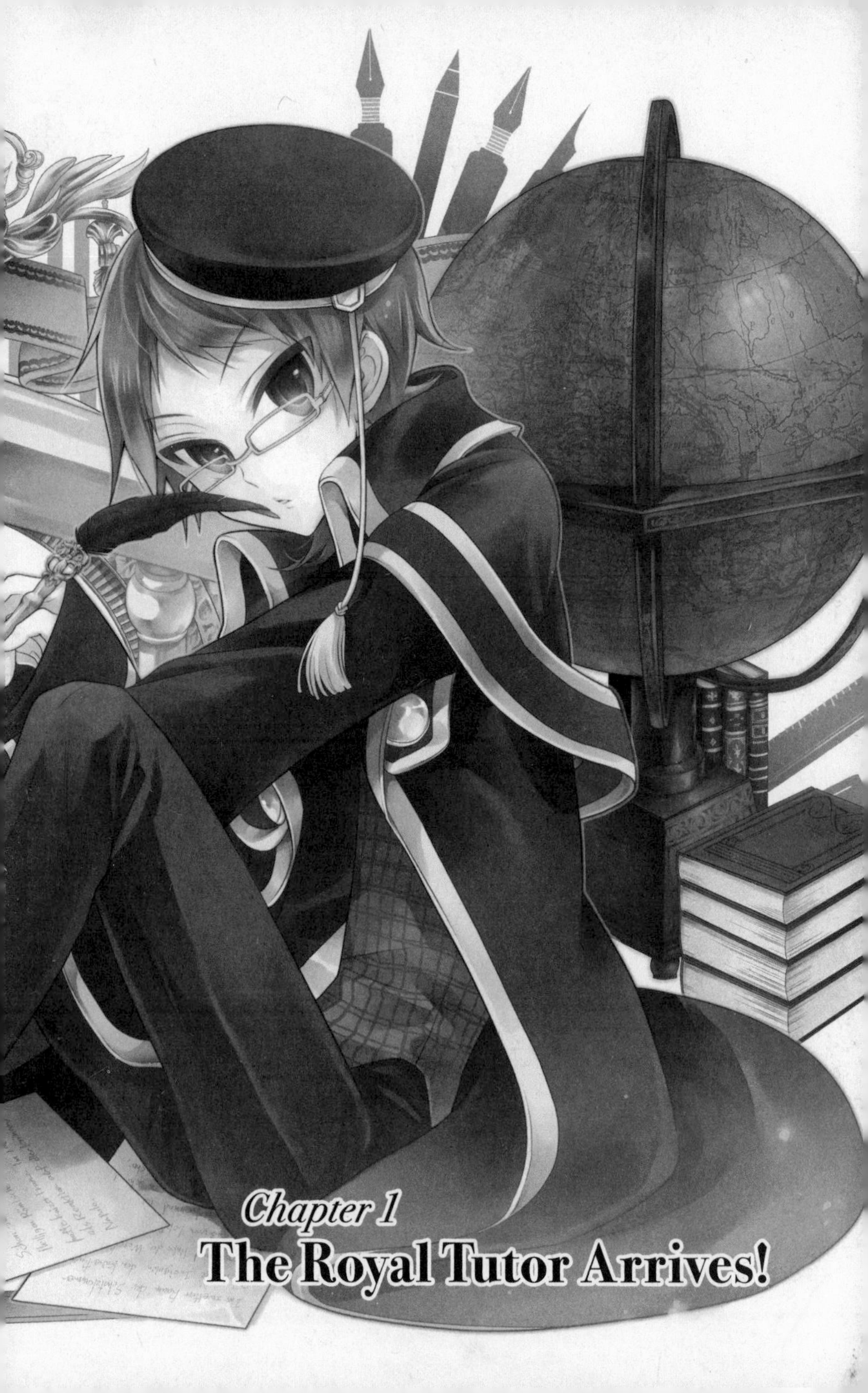
Chapter 1
The Royal Tutor Arrives!

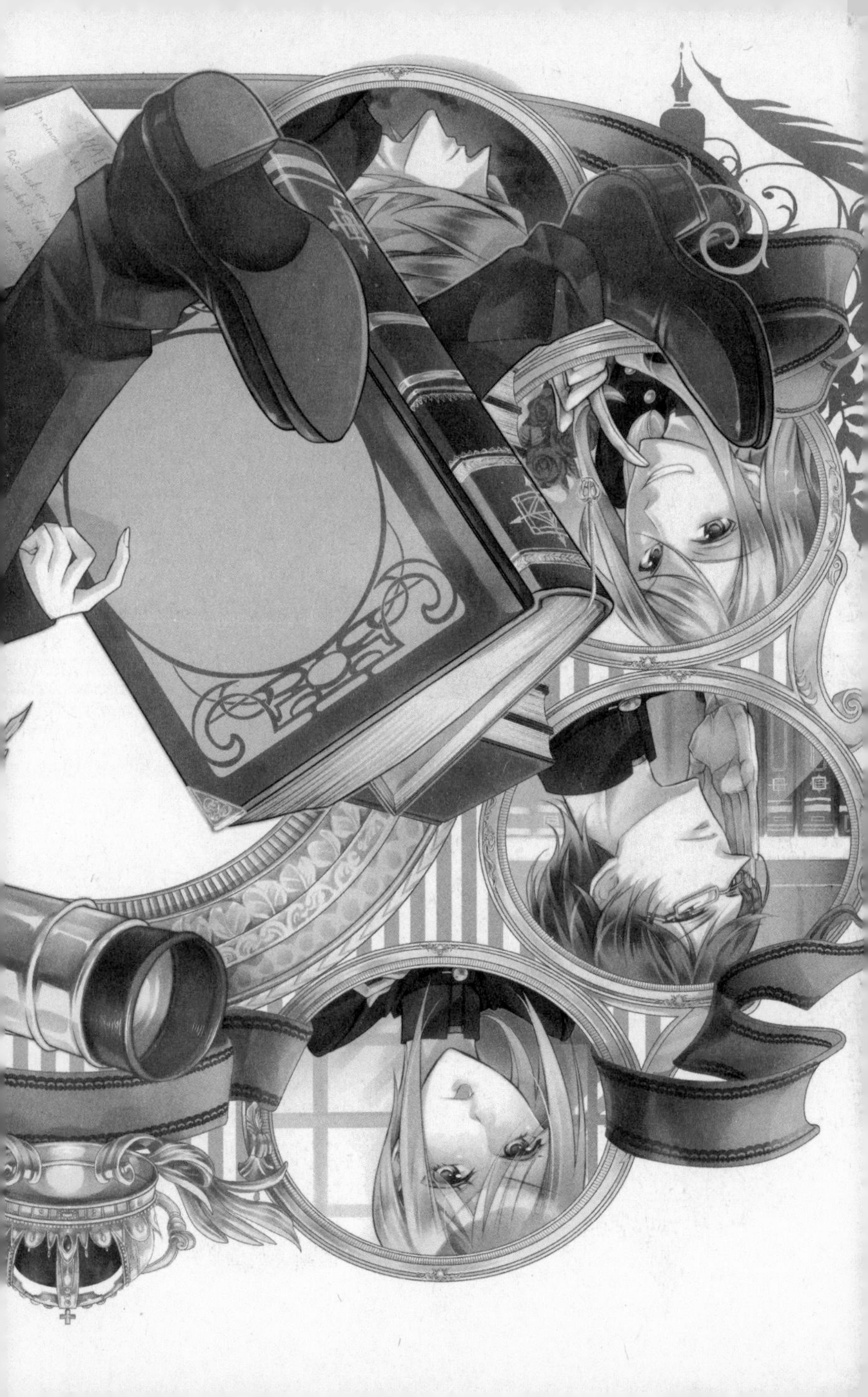

WIENNER, CAPITAL OF THE KINGDOM OF GRANZ-REICH

CLATTER
CLATTER
CLATTER
KACHK

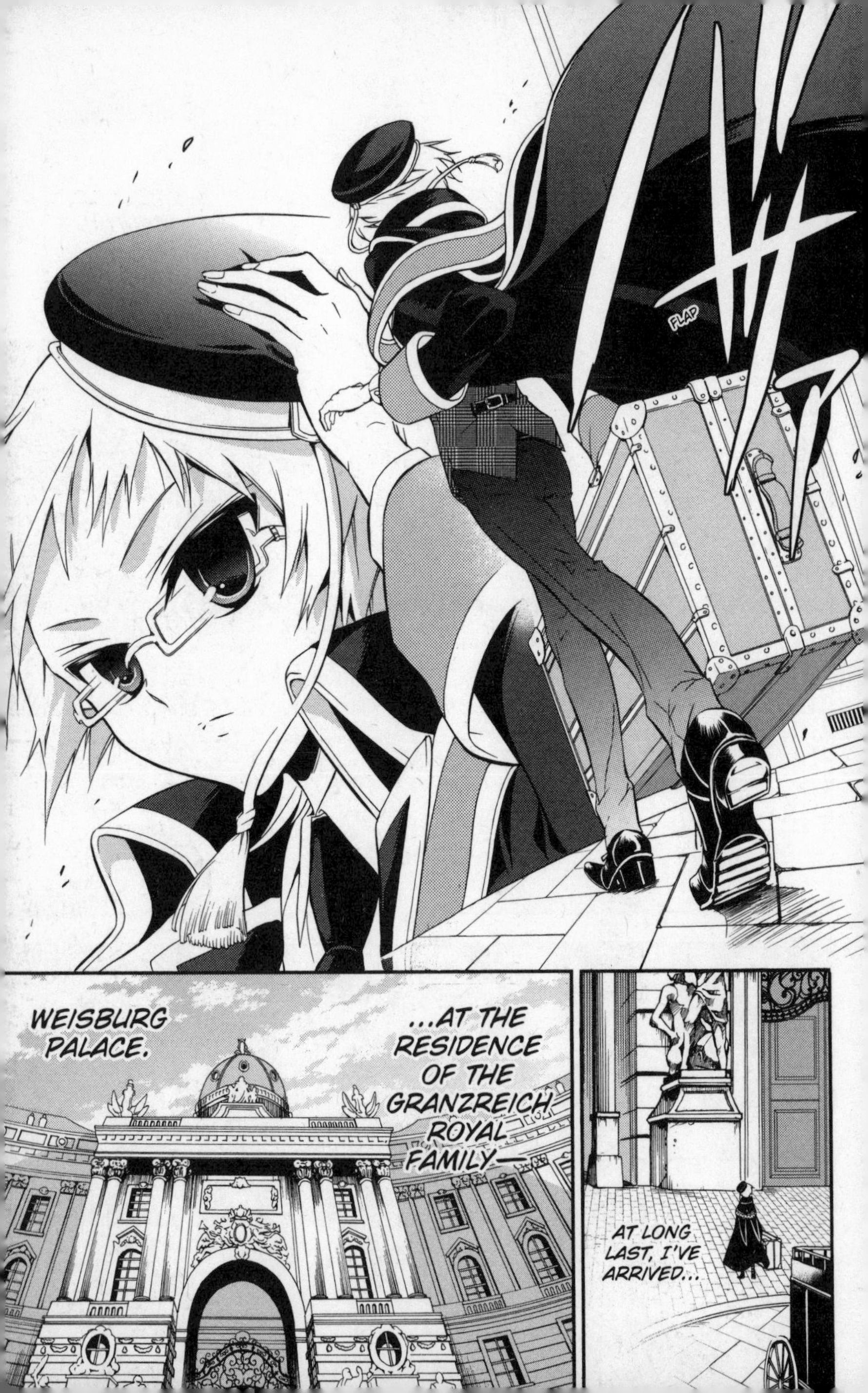
FLAP
WEISBURG PALACE.
...AT THE RESIDENCE OF THE GRANZREICH ROYAL FAMILY—
AT LONG LAST, I'VE ARRIVED...

STARTING TODAY, THIS IS WHERE I SHALL LIVE AND WORK AS ROYAL TUTOR...
ON THE PATH TO ACHIEVING MY PERSONAL GOALS...

...THIS IS MY FIRST STEP!
FWSH

......
SCUTTLE SCUTTLE SCUTTLE
ちま ちま ちま ちま

NOT SO FAST, LAD!
!?
GRAB
HIS FIRST STEP, IMPEDED.

YOU! YOU, LAD!!
YOU CAN'T GO WALTZING INTO THE PALACE AS YOU LIKE!
...?
"LAD"? OF WHOM DO YOU SPEAK?
きょろきょろ
GLANCE GLANCE
I AM NOT "WALTZ-ING IN."
I HAVE A ROYAL SUMMONS FROM HIS MAJESTY THE KING, IF YOU WISH TO SEE IT.
HUH?

I SHOULD HAVE IN-TRODUCED MYSELF.
I AM THE NEW ROYAL TUTOR, HEINE—
OH! YOU'RE PROFESSOR HEINE'S SON!

PAPA'S TRAVELING COMPANION, ARE YOU?
THERE'S A GOOD LAD.
OHH, IS THAT RIGHT? WAIT FOR YOUR PAPA TO ARRIVE, AND HE'LL TAKE YOU INSIDE WITH HIM!
HAHA HAHAHAHA HAHA
HA HA

HRUMPH...

HMM? I DON'T SEE HIS CARRIAGE...
HUH?
TO THINK I WOULD BE STOPPED AT THE GATES...
HOW WILL I CLEAR UP THIS MIS-UNDER-STAND-ING?
SLUMP
TAK
WHEREVER COULD PROFES-SOR HEINE BE...?
GLANCE GLANCE

HER ROYAL HIGHNESS THE QUEEN MOTHER!
KNEEL

WHY, THERE HE IS!
PRO-FESSOR HEINE!
!?
SHALL WE? I'LL SHOW YOU INSIDE.
I WOULD BE GREATLY OBLIGED.

"P-PROFESSOR HEINE," SHE SAID...
Y... ...YOU DON'T THINK HE'S...?

PARDON THE LATE INTRODUCTION.
I AM HEINE WITTGENSTEIN, AND FROM TODAY FORTH, I AM TO BE EMPLOYED HERE AS THE ROYAL TUTOR.
I'LL HAVE YOU KNOW, DESPITE MY APPEARANCE...
...I AM A FULL-GROWN ADULT.

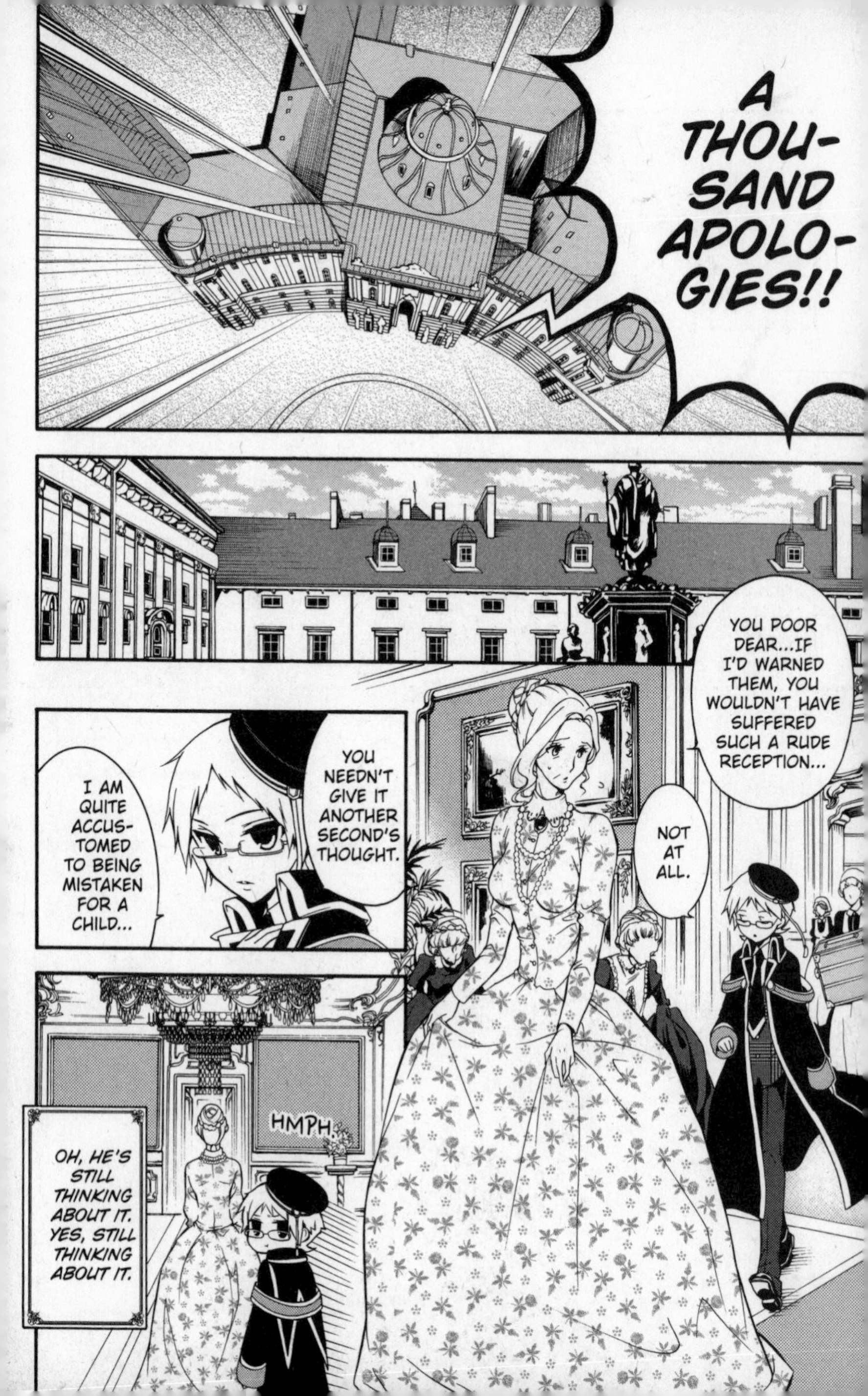
A THOUSAND APOLOGIES!!
YOU POOR DEAR...IF I'D WARNED THEM, YOU WOULDN'T HAVE SUFFERED SUCH A RUDE RECEPTION...
NOT AT ALL.
YOU NEEDN'T GIVE IT ANOTHER SECOND'S THOUGHT.
I AM QUITE ACCUSTOMED TO BEING MISTAKEN FOR A CHILD...
HMPH.
OH, HE'S STILL THINKING ABOUT IT. YES, STILL THINKING ABOUT IT.

...I MUST ADMIT THAT RECEIVING A LETTER IN HIS MAJESTY THE KING'S OWN HAND...
...HAS LEFT ME QUITE STUN-NED.
EH?
I STILL CANNOT BELIEVE THAT A MERE COMMONER SUCH AS MYSELF HAS BEEN CALLED TO THE ROYAL PALACE...
NON-SENSE.
THE KING HAS HAD NOTHING BUT PRAISE FOR YOUR EXCEL-LENCE AS AN EDUCATOR.
IS THIS NOT A SPECIAL EXCEPTION IN RECOGNITION OF YOUR ABILITY?
......
A SPECIAL EXCEP-TION...
"HERR HEINE WITTGENSTEIN —
"AS KING OF GRANZ-REICH...
"...I INVITE YOU TO THE PALACE AS THE ROYAL TUTOR."

TO BE BLESSED WITH ONE PRINCESS AND FIVE PRINCES.
"MY ELDEST SON IS A FINE CANDIDATE FOR THE CROWN.
"YET I CANNOT DISCOUNT THE ONE-IN-A-MILLION CHANCE THAT AN ILL FATE AWAITS HIM.
"THUS, I WOULD APPOINT YOU AS TUTOR TO HIS FOUR YOUNGER BROTHERS...
"...TO GROOM THEM INTO WORTHY POTENTIAL SUCCESSORS TO THE THRONE.
"AS I SEE IT, THEY ARE STILL UNFIT TO RULE.
"TO PREVENT THE DIFFERENCE IN ABILITIES AMONG INDI-VIDUAL TUTORS FROM CAUSING UNFAIRNESS IN THEIR GROWTH...
"...I WOULD HAVE YOU OVERSEE THEIR STUDIES WITH AN EQUAL HAND AS THEIR SOLE TUTOR."

"IF ANY OF THEM GROW TO RIVAL THEIR ELDEST BROTHER IN WORTHINESS FOR THE CROWN...
"...THEN AT THAT TIME"—
....

CLASP
!?
LOOOOM
PROFES-SOR!
MY LITTLE PRINCES...
I BEG OF YOU—TREAT THEM DEARLY!

??
...YOU SEE...
THE PRINCES' TUTORS ARE ALWAYS SO QUICK TO LEAVE.
I CAN'T FATHOM WHY...IT'S THE MOST CURIOUS THING...
RESIG-NATION

FORGIVE ME, BUT COULD THE PROBLEM LIE WITH THE PRINCES THEM-SELVES...?
SHOCK

N-NEVER!
WHY, THEY'RE SUCH GOOD BOYS.
IT MUST BE THAT THEY'RE ALREADY SO PERFECT, THEIR TUTORS SIMPLY HAD NOTHING TO TEACH THEM...
YES, I'M SURE OF IT...!
INSTEAD OF A DOTING PARENT, IT'S A DOTING GRAND-PARENT...

I SUSPECT I'VE BEEN TASKED WITH MORE TROUBLE THAN I WAS LED TO EXPECT...
......
I WELCOME THE CHALLENGE. FULFILLING THIS DUTY SATISFACTORILY IS MY ONLY CONCERN.
GLINT

THE PRINCES ARE WAITING BEYOND THESE DOORS.
I'LL LEAVE THEM TO YOU, PROFESSOR.
KACHAK
NO MATTER HOW PROBLEMATIC THE PRINCES MAY PROVE TO BE, I'LL GROOM THEM INTO PROPER ROYALS.
IT IS MY DUTY AS A PRO-FESSIONAL EDUCATOR!
SHFF
CREEEEAK

SLAM

......

TAK
TAK

KNEEL

FREUT MICH, YOUR ROYAL HIGHNESSES.
MY NAME IS HEINE WITTGEN-STEIN.

FROM TODAY FORTH, I SHALL BE YOUR TUTOR.

SWSH
WHOOOSH
—NH!

ICH FREUE MICH, SIE KENNEN ZU LERNEN...
<IT'S A PLEASURE TO MEET YOU...>

...HERR WITTGENSTEIN.

ザァァァ
RUSTLE
.........!

BRIMMING WITH NOBILITY... AND VIRTUE...
THIS... IS WHAT DEFINES A PRINCE...

LEAN
HOW BREATH-TAKING...
AS THOUGH HE STEPPED OUT OF A PAINTING... A PERFECT PRINCE...
WE WELCOME YOU WITH OPEN ARMS, HERR WITTGENSTEIN...

...HARD-LY.
DID YOU HONESTLY EXPECT A WARM WELCOME FROM ME?

!!?

A SUDDEN, INEXPLICA-BLE...
...VEN-OMOUS LOOK.

BEFORE MAKING THE ERROR OF THINKING YOURSELF IMPORTANT, LET ME WARN YOU.

NO MATTER WHAT MY FATHER'S ORDERS, YOU'RE NOTHING MORE THAN A TEACHER.
A MERE COMMONER.
SIT
I, FOURTH PRINCE OF THE KINGDOM OF GRANZREICH...
...LEONHARD VON GRANZREICH...
...WILL NOT ALLOW YOU TO ORDER ME AROUND.
UNDERSTOOD?

......
HE MAY LOOK BREATH-TAKINGLY BEAUTIFUL...
...BUT ONCE HE OPENS HIS MOUTH, HE'S BREATH-TAKINGLY HAUGHTY.
AS PROUD AS MOUNT EVEREST IS TALL... PROUD PRINCE EVEREST...
TMP TMP
TEEEEACH! GOTCHA!
YANK
!?

OOH, OOH, TEACH! ARE YOU REALLY A GROWN-UP?
WOOOW! YOU'RE SO LIGHT AND TIIINY!
HAVE YOU ALWAYS BEEN LIKE THIS? EXACTLY HOW TALL ARE YOU!?
TELL MEEE!
... EXCUSE ME...
DANGLE
DANGLE
DANGLE

DAMMIT, LICHT!
I WASN'T DONE TALKING!
YOU CAN'T HOG HIM, LEONIE!
I WANNA TALK TO THE TINY TEACHER TOO!
EX-CUSE ME...
HUMPH!
HE CALLED ME "TINY" TWICE!
WHOOPSIES! I DIDN'T INTRODUCE MYSELF, HUH?
DROP
I'M LICHT VON GRANZ—
AHHH, MY FULL NAME'S SO LOOONG. "LICHT" IS GOOD ENOUGH!
JUST CALL ME "LICHIE," 'KAY? ♪
"LICHIE"... FROM "LICHT"...?
YAY!

HOW FRIENDLY THIS PRINCE SEEMS. YOU WOULDN'T THINK HIM A ROYAL.
STARE
POMF

TEACH... HAVE MY GOOD LOOKS HYPNO-TIZED YOU?
GO AHEAD. HAVE A LONG LOOK. TAKE IT ALL IN. HEH... I'M SO SEXY, IT'S SINFUL.
SHIMMER
....

SINFULLY SHAMELESS IS WHAT YOU ARE!
WHAP
YOWCH!

WH-WHAT'S YOUR PROBLEM, BRUNIE!?
THE RUCKUS MY YOUNGER BROTHERS ARE MAKING IS TRULY APPALLING.
OH, NOT AT ALL.
AS THE THIRD-ELDEST BROTHER, BRUNO, I SINCERELY APOLOGIZE FOR THEIR BEHAVIOR.

...BY THE WAY, I TOOK THE LIBERTY OF PERUSING WHAT MATERIALS I COULD GATHER REGARDING YOUR BACKGROUND...
...BUT NOTHING WHATSOEVER WAS WRITTEN CONCERNING YOUR ACADEMIC RECORD.
WHERE IN THE WORLD DID YOU ATTEND UNIVERSITY?

NO-WHERE.
PAR-DON ME?
I HAVE NOT GONE TO UNIVERSITY.
......
...IS THAT SO.

...? HE'S PROPERLY POLITE...
...BUT HIS GAZE GREW STRANGELY COLD JUST NOW...

ALLOW ME TO INTRODUCE KAI, THE SECOND-ELDEST PRINCE.
BROTHER, YOU SHOULD AT LEAST GREET THE NEW TUTOR.

...TEA...
...EET
Y...
?
...I COULDN'T HEAR HIM.
THEN HE GLOWERED AT ME...
TURN
GLARE

ALTHOUGH IT WASN'T WITHOUT A FEW ODD MOMENTS...
...I'VE GREETED EACH OF THEM, IN ANY CASE.
NOW, THEN, I'LL GET STRAIGHT TO THE MATTER AT HAND.
SO THAT I MAY DETER-MINE THE DIRECTION YOUR INDIVIDUAL LESSONS SHALL TAKE...
...I SHOULD LIKE TO INTERVIEW EACH OF YOU PRIVATELY.
THAT WON'T BE NECESSARY.
SHFF

NONE OF US WANTS A TUTOR...!

I DETEST TEACHERS MORE THAN ANYTHING ELSE IN THE WORLD!

I'LL NEVER ACKNOWLEDGE YOU AS OUR TUTOR!!

I'M AFRAID I MUST AGREE.
IN MY SCHOOL, I AM ALWAYS THE TOP STUDENT.
I DO NOT REQUIRE A SO-CALLED "TUTOR" WHO HAS NEVER EVEN STUDIED AT UNIVERSITY.
YOU GUYS THINK SO?
WELL, IF MY BIG BROTHERS ARE AGAINST IT, THEN I AM TOOOO.
NOT THAT IT MAKES A DIFFERENCE TO ME EITHER WAY!
......
......

IT ALL MAKES SENSE NOW...
I FINALLY SEE WHY SO MANY TUTORS FLED FROM THEIR POSTS HERE.
THE PRINCES SHUNNED AND REJECTED THEM ON A UNITED FRONT, MERELY FOR BEING TEACHERS.
THE PRINCES WOULDN'T ACCEPT THEIR TUTELAGE IN THE SLIGHTEST...
... KH...
CLENCH
YOUR HIGHNESSES HAVE MADE YOUR FEELINGS MOST CLEAR...

NOW, THEN.
WHOM SHALL I INTERVIEW FIRST?

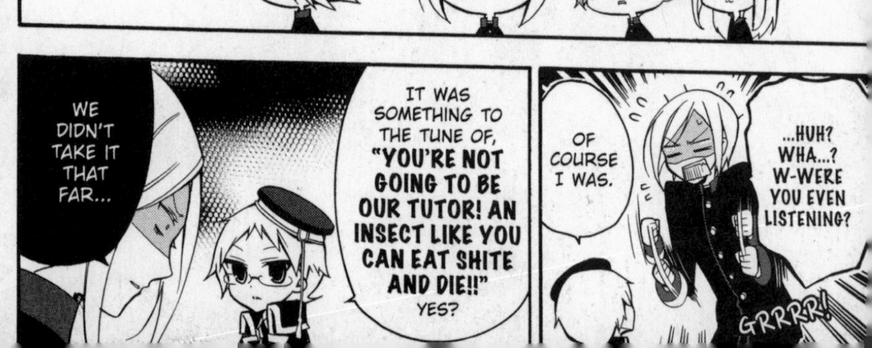
...HUH? WHA...? W-WERE YOU EVEN LISTENING?
OF COURSE I WAS.
GRRRR!
IT WAS SOMETHING TO THE TUNE OF, "YOU'RE NOT GOING TO BE OUR TUTOR! AN INSECT LIKE YOU CAN EAT SHITE AND DIE!!" YES?
WE DIDN'T TAKE IT THAT FAR...

I AM HERE ONLY TO FULFILL MY ROLE AS ROYAL TUTOR.
YOUR HIGHNESSES' MOODS HAVE NO BEARING ON THIS.
CRACK
THE TASK OF A TEACHER IS TO EDUCATE HIS STUDENTS.

NOT...
...TO CURRY THEIR FAVOR.
—GH!

Chapter 2
Interview with a Prince I

...INSOLENT CUR.
YOU REFUSE TO LEAVE OUR PALACE, DO YOU?
....
TOO BAD. IF THE FOUR OF US GO ON STRIKE...
...FATHER WILL HAVE TO RECON-SIDER...
WE BROTHERS WILL BAND TOGETHER...
FWIP
...TO SEE YOU OUSTED FROM THE POST OF ROYAL TUTOR!

TIK
TIK
TIK
...AH.
GONG
OH DRAT! IT'S ALREADY THIS LATE!?
WHIRL
HUH?

SORRY, LEONIE! I HAVE GUESTS WAITING IN MY ROOM!
YOU CAN TAKE CARE OF THIS!
ZOOM
WHAT !!?

LICHT... THAT STUPID LITTLE...
MORE WOMEN, I'M SURE.
HOW UNSEEMLY FOR A ROYAL...
HAAH...
I-IT'S NO MATTER. I WASN'T EXPECTING ANYTHING FROM HIM IN THE FIRST PLACE...
DEAREST BROTHER BRUNO!
YOU AND I WILL CHASE AWAY THIS IMPUDENT TEACHER TOGETHER —

...I AM INTRIGUED. YOU'RE THE FIRST TEACHER TO CHALLENGE US HEAD-ON.
I'LL CONSENT TO THIS INTERVIEW OF YOURS.
HUH!?

HOWEVER, I AM PENNING A PAPER THAT REQUIRES MY IMMEDIATE ATTENTION.
COME TO MY QUARTERS AFTER YOU'VE INTERVIEWED LEONHARD.

AS YOU WISH, YOUR HIGHNESS.
STAGGER
WH-WHY...? DEAREST BROTHER BRUNO...

......
...U-UM... ELDER BROTH-ER...?
PEEK

STRIDE
STMP
STMP
STMP
TOO FAST!

....

ぽつーん
ALONE
……
ABANDONED BY ALL OF YOUR BROTHERS…
WHAT A PITY, PRINCE LEONHARD.
URGH!
SH-SHUT UP… DON'T PITY ME…

THERE, THERE. SIT DOWN AND SPEAK WITH ME. YOU SEE? YOU ARE NOT ALONE.
I! DON'T! WANT! TO!
すすす
SHUFFLE
YOU LISTEN GOOD!! I DO NOT NEED A TUTOR! NOT NOW, NOT EVER!
GOT THAT!?
YES, YES, VERY WELL.
LET US TAKE THIS TO YOUR HIGHNESS'S QUARTERS.
ずるずるずる
DRAG DRAG DRAG

THE FOURTH PRINCE, LEONHARD. FIFTEEN YEARS OF AGE.
A VISION OF A PRINCE, HIS IS CONSIDERED THE MOST BEAUTIFUL FACE ON THE WESTERN CONTINENT. THEY CALL HIM THE "WHITE LILY OF GRANZREICH."
YET HE NEVER BOASTS ABOUT THE APPEARANCE WITH WHICH HE HAS BEEN BLESSED. HE IS A MAN OF CHARACTER, ALWAYS HUMBLE, ALWAYS KINDHEARTED.
THAT DESCRIBES PRINCE LEONHARD, ACCORDING TO OFFICIAL DOCUMENTS, NEWSPAPER CLIPPINGS, AND RUMORS IN THE CITY. HOWEVER...
GLANCE
ちらっ

WHAT? YOU GOT SOMETHING TO SAY TO ME, COMMONER?
GLARE
THE REAL PRINCE LEONHARD IS AS ARROGANT AS MOUNT EVEREST IS TALL.

DON'T GET THE WRONG IDEA. I DECIDED TO LET YOU INTO MY ROOM. THAT'S IT.
THAT DOESN'T MEAN I'M WELCOMING YOU AS A TUTOR.
I'M ONLY GOING ALONG WITH THIS INTERVIEW NONSENSE ON A WHIM.
I UNDER-STAND.

THE MAIN PURPOSE OF THESE ONE-ON-ONE INTERVIEWS IS TO FAMILIARIZE MYSELF WITH EACH OF THE PRINCES' DISPOSITIONS.

I HAVE ONE OTHER IMPORTANT GOAL—
TO GIVE THEM A COMPETENCY TEST SO THAT I MAY GAUGE THEIR ACADEMIC LEVELS.
SHP

IF I ASK HIM TO TAKE THIS TEST, I DOUBT HE'LL AGREE EASILY.
I'LL TAKE IT OUT AFTER CHATTING WITH HIM A BIT.
STARE

MRRRM...

HMPH!

YOUR HIGHNESS, YOU DID NOT CARE FOR ME ON FIRST SIGHT, DID YOU?
CLEARLY.

......

I TOLD YOU— I DESPISE TEACHERS.
YES, BUT THAT'S HARDLY REASON TO—
SHUT UP!
BAM

TO ME, HOLDING THE TITLE OF "TEACHER" ITSELF DESERVES UNRESERVED DISDAIN...!
STUPID TEACHERS...
STUPID TEACHERS...!
JAB
I HATE STUPID TEACHERS ALMOST AS MUCH AS I HATE CARROTS AND BELL PEPPERS!!
WHY AM I BEING COMPARED TO VEGETABLES?

YOU DISLIKE CARROTS AND BELL PEPPERS, YOUR HIGH-NESS?
AH!
...NH!
......!

TH-THE BITTER TASTE, THE SMELL...
I'VE NEVER BEEN ABLE TO STOMACH THEM FOR AS LONG AS I CAN REMEMBER.
WH-WHAT OF IT, HMM?
FWIP
YOUR HIGHNESS IS UNEX-PECTEDLY CHILDISH...

HOW DARE YOU!? I'LL HAVE YOU KNOW, I'M FIFTEEN YEARS OLD!
I AM A MODEL GROWN-UP!
WHY, AS I KNOW THAT I MUSTN'T SPOIL MY APPETITE FOR DINNER, I RESIST EATING TORTE IN THE EVENINGS, AND IT'S MY FAVORITE!
HOW GROWN-UP IS THAT!?
HO HO HO!
HNNGH... WANT TO... EAT IT... MUST... RESIST...
YOUR HIGHNESS IS INDEED A MODEL (FOR CHILDREN) TO FOLLOW...

MAY I INQUIRE AS TO WHY YOUR DISLIKE FOR TEACHERS IS SO POWERFUL?
HMPH! YOU WOULDN'T UNDER-STAND.
I CANNOT RECTIFY THE ISSUE WITHOUT KNOWING THE REASON YOU FEEL THIS WAY.

I BELIEVE THERE SHOULD BE A BOND OF TRUST BETWEEN TEACHER AND STUDENT—
TEACHERS CAN'T BE TRUSTED!
......
NONE OF MY TEACHERS HAS EVER CARED ABOUT ME, THEIR STUDENT ...
THEY WERE ALL TOO BUSY TRYING TO GAIN MY FATHER'S FAVOR...
I SEE. HE'S STRUGGLING WITH COMPLICATED FEELINGS ARISING FROM HIS STATION AS PRINCE.
BUT MORE THAN ANY-THING...

...I DETEST ...
... STÜDYING.

THEREFORE, TEACHERS... THOSE WHO FORCE ME TO STUDY...
...ARE THE ENEMY!
HIS FEELINGS ARE NOT SO COMPLICATED, AFTER ALL.
WHAT MANNER OF LESSONS DID YOUR HIGHNESS HAVE WITH THE PREVIOUS ROYAL TUTORS, THEN?
IF YOU DISLIKE STUDYING TO THIS EXTENT, THEY MUST HAVE ARRANGED MATERIAL THAT WAS EASY TO LEARN...

I RAN FROM THEM ALL.
DOOM
HOW DIRECT.

SOMETIMES I WOULD SPRINT ON FOOT...
ZOOOOM
HUFF! HAFF!
HUFF!
TUTOR →
GALLOP
WHEEZE!
HUFF!
HUFF!
TUTOR →

THESE ARE ALL THE TROPHIES I'VE WON THANKS TO THE TECHNIQUE AND STRENGTH I WAS ABLE TO HONE IN MY FLIGHTS.
STUFFED
...THE YOUNG PRINCELING IS NOT AS INTELLIGENT AS HE APPEARS.
MY, MY.
HE ONLY HAS A HEAD FOR SPORTS.

HEH. WELL, HEINE? HAS MY ABILITY LEFT YOU QUIVERING IN FRIGHT?
...IN A MANNER OF SPEAK-ING, YES.

IF HIS AVERSION TO STUDYING IS SO GREAT...
...HE'S LIKELY TO TAKE OFF RUNNING WHEN I PRESENT HIM WITH THIS TEST.
...

YOUR HIGHNESS, ON OCCASION, SURELY THE MOOD TO STUDY—
CLATTER

—DOES NOT STIR WITHIN YOU.
SIIIIT
...
...WHAT ARE YOU SCHEM-ING?
NOTHING. NOTHING AT ALL.
......
......

YOUR HIGHNESS, I HAVE A POP QUIZ FOR—
WHOOSH

SWOOP
!!?
OHO...YOU ACTUALLY MANAGED TO KEEP UP WITH ME... NOT BAD...!
TENSE
TENSE
ENOUGH OF THAT. HURRY UP AND TAKE YOUR TEST.

THERE'S NO NEED TO BE NERVOUS. IT'S ONLY THE MOST BASIC OF QUESTIONS IN LANGUAGE ARTS, ARITHMETIC, AND OTHER FUNDAMENTAL SUBJECTS.
IF YOU WOULD RELAX...

NOOO! I CAN'T BELIEVE YOU WERE HIDING A TEST! I KNEW I COULD NEVER TRUST A TEACHERRR! MOVE IT— KOFF! HAGKH! (CHOKED)
SOB
SOB
SOB
YOU NEEDN'T PUT UP SUCH A DRAMATIC STRUGGLE...
DISGUSTING...

TCH! IF THAT'S HOW YOU WANT TO PLAY IT, I'LL FORCE MY WAY OUT WITH A RUNNING START—
BUMP

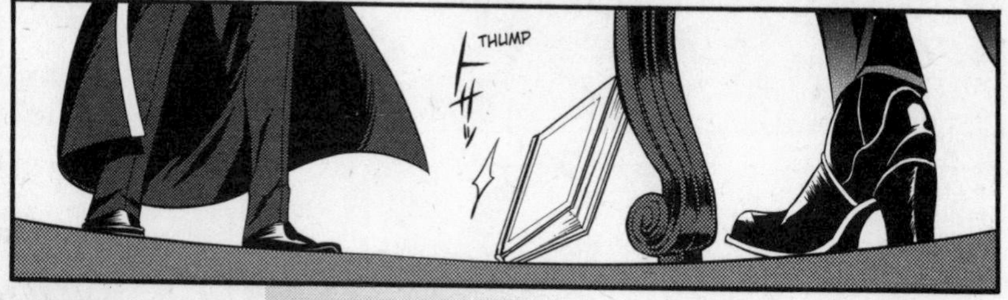
THUMP

!!!
Tegebuch
Diary

?
A BOOK FELL.
ACK! Y-YOU IDIOT!

FLIP
"Today's disaster—
Once again, I couldn't say a proper 'thank you' to the maid who brought me my melange. I'm a hopeless, worthless excuse for a human being. An utter waste. A piece of trash. I'm not worthy to go on living..."

WHAT A FRIGHTFULLY NEGATIVE DIARY...

"Today's disaster—
I ruined a book I borrowed from dearest brother Bruno.
I want to die."
THIS IS... A DIARY OF REGRETS.
HE BEGINS EACH ENTRY DECLARING THE DAY A DISASTER...
YOU KEEP THIS KIND OF JOURNAL, DO YOU, PRINCE LEONHARD?
STARE
U-UM...! N-NO... THAT'S...

THAT'S MY LITTLE BROTHER'S DIARY! YES!
LICHT MUST HAVE FORGOTTEN IT HERE IN MY ROOM!
BAM

Leonhard

G-GIVE IT!
GIVE IT BACK! IT'S PRIVATE...!
OH, THAT WON'T DO. NAUGHTY STUDENTS WHO DITCH THEIR TESTS MUST BE PUNISHED.
DRAG
DRAG
"AUGUST 10. TODAY'S DISASTER—I PICKED THE PEPPERS OUT OF THE GOULASH WE HAD FOR DINNER..."
ACK! WHAT ARE YOU—? YOU CAN'T READ THAT OUT LOUD HERE...!
GLANCE
"MARCH 29. TODAY'S DISASTER—"
AH!
COME ON...S-STO...
NH...!
"ONCE AGAIN, I BOLTED FROM MY LESSONS. WHY AM I SUCH A—"
O-OKAY! FINE! I'LL TAKE YOUR STUPID TEST!
MURMUR
MURMUR
WHAT?
WHAT'S ALL THIS NOW?
WAAAH!
I SWEAR I'LL DO IT! JUST STOP, YOU SADIST!!

ONCE HE MANAGES TO BEGIN, HE CONFRONTS THE TASK AT HAND WITH SURPRISING DILIGENCE.
ALL THROUGH TEARS...
UHN!
GUHN!
HIC!
SWISH
OH DEAR. THE PRINCE'S DIARY...
FLUTTER
......
WHAT'S THIS...?
"PHYSICAL ACTIVITIES ARE MY ONLY STRENGTH. EVEN MY SOCIAL SKILLS ARE LACKING.
"I'M ALWAYS SO QUICK TO FLEE FROM MY STUDIES AND OTHER THINGS I DON'T CARE FOR. BUT...
"...I'D LIKE TO THINK THAT IF I RECORD MY MISTAKES IN THIS DIARY, I CAN IMPROVE UPON MYSELF LITTLE BY LITTLE."

"THEN MAYBE ONE DAY...
"...I CAN BE AS AMAZING AS MY BROTHER BRUNO."
....
IT'S DIFFICULT TO IMAGINE PRINCE LEONHARD BEING SO SENSITIVE...
...GIVEN THE EVEREST-HIGH HAUGH-TINESS HE SO DRAMATICALLY DISPLAYS.

COULD IT BE THAT HE HIDES A WEAKER SIDE OF HIMSELF BEHIND THAT MASK OF BRAVADO?
DEEP DOWN, HE MAY BE BUT A TIMID CHILD...

THINKING OF IT THAT WAY, YOU COULD SAY THERE'S A BIT OF INNOCENT CHARM ABOUT HIM.
STARE

MRRRM...

HMPH!
OR NO CHARM AT ALL.

GOOD. I SHALL TAKE YOUR ANSWER SHEET, THEN.
SLUMP
ぐったり

PLEASE BE PRESENT IN THE SAME PARLOR AS EARLIER AT FOUR IN THE AFTERNOON.
I'LL BE SHARING THE RESULTS OF YOUR TEST AND MY PLANS FOR YOUR FUTURE STUDIES.

HMPH...! YEAH, RIGHT.
YOU CAN'T BREAK DOWN MY RESOLVE...
I DON'T NEED...ANY TUTOR...!

IS THAT SO?
EXCUSE ME!

HE LEFT ...!?
SHOCK

NOT THAT I WANTED HIM TO HANG AROUND!
BUT HOW HE WAS SO QUICK TO LEAVE...IT'S PERPLEXING... EXASPERATING...
DAMN HIM! HE... HE'S NOT TAKING ME SERIOUS-LY!!
AAH!
FINE! WE'LL SEE HOW THAT FOUL HEINE LIKES IT WHEN I VOICE MY PROTESTS TO FATHER!
GRAAA

KNOCK
KNOCK
JOLT
HEINE!?
HATE DIARY

KACHAK
PARDON ME, YOUR ROYAL HIGH-NESS.

I BROUGHT WHAT YOU REQUESTED.
COME AGAIN ...?

I DON'T RECALL ASKING FOR ANYTHING.
B-BUT I WAS TOLD TO BRING THIS TO YOU...

...BY HERR WITTGEN-STEIN.
Ich danke Ihnen sehr für Ihre Mühe
Heine
Thank you for your effort.

W-WELL, I SUPPOSE I'LL LET HIM OFF WITHOUT COMPLAIN-ING TO FATHER...
B-BUT I'M NOT DOING ANYTHING ELSE HE SAYS!
MM...I DO LOVE TORTE...
I'M ONLY SPOILING YOU THIS ONCE.

THE ROYAL TUTOR

Chapter 3
Interview with a Prince II

THE THIRD BROTHER, BRUNO. SIXTEEN YEARS OF AGE.
A PRINCE POSSESSING EXTRAORDINARY INTELLIGENCE, HE HAS BEEN LAUDED AS A GENIUS WITH A BRILLIANT MIND FROM A VERY YOUNG AGE.
HE HAS ALREADY PUBLISHED NUMEROUS THESES. THOUGH STILL YOUNG, HE IS A BUDDING SCHOLAR SPECIALIZING IN SOCIOLOGY AND PHILOSOPHY.
HMM. CONSIDERING THE PITY THAT IS PRINCE LEONHARD...
...I WILL NOT BE SO QUICK TO TRUST THESE NOTES ON HIS BROTHER.
A "PITY"

KNOCK
KNOCK
KACHAK
WELCOME, HERR WITTGEN-STEIN.
SIT THERE.
MY WORD...
WHAT AN IMPECCA-BLY TIDY ROOM.
I'D LIKE YOU TO TAKE A COMPETENCY TEST.
CER-TAINLY.
SWSH
SWSH
THAT WENT TOO SMOOTHLY ...
THE CONTRAST IS UNSET-TLING.
EARLIER
HURRY UP AND TAKE IT.
NOOO! NO TESTS!

I REALIZE THIS IS OUT OF THE BLUE...
...BUT I WILL HAVE TO TEST YOUR ABILITIES AS WELL.
TEST ME?
YES. TO EVALUATE HOW LEARNED A ROYAL TUTOR WHO HAS NEVER STUDIED AT UNIVERSITY COULD POSSIBLY BE.
MY KNOWLEDGE HAS ALWAYS SURPASSED THAT OF MY TUTORS IN ALL AREAS OF STUDY.
....
IF YOU ARE NO EXCEPTION, I SHALL HAVE TO DEMAND THAT YOU RESIGN POSTHASTE.

ABRUPTLY CHALLENGING ME, AND WITH SUCH BLATANT HOSTILITY...
HIS EXCEPTIONAL INTELLIGENCE MAKES IT THAT MUCH MORE DIFFICULT TO GAIN HIS TRUST. I'LL NEED TO EXERCISE DISCRETION.
I SHOULD DECLINE THIS PROPOSAL FOR NOW TO AVOID STIRRING UP ANY UNNECESSARY FRICTION...

I HAVE ONE MORE CONCERN.
I NEVER IMAGINED THAT THE NEW ROYAL TUTOR WOULD BE THIS... SMALL.
PRIK

AS YOU WISH.
DO YOUR WORST.
HRMPH.
...? HE'S BECOME STRANGELY COMPETI-TIVE...
OH, PROFESSOR. HOW IMMATURE.

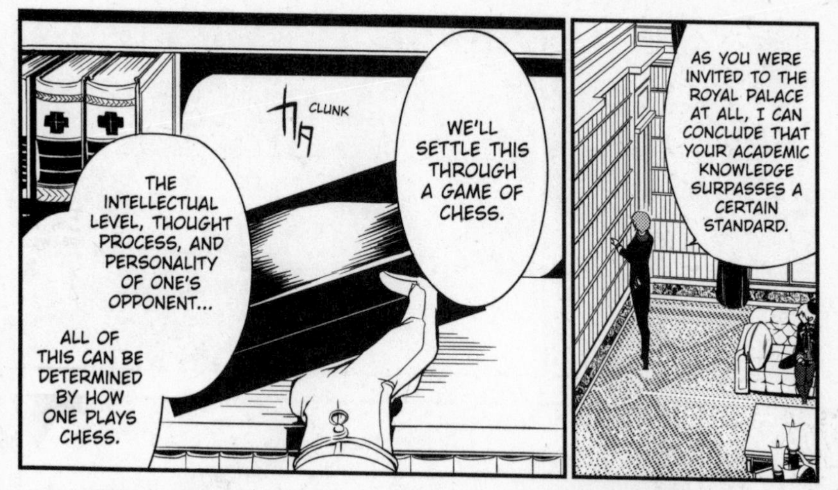
AS YOU WERE INVITED TO THE ROYAL PALACE AT ALL, I CAN CONCLUDE THAT YOUR ACADEMIC KNOWLEDGE SURPASSES A CERTAIN STANDARD.
WE'LL SETTLE THIS THROUGH A GAME OF CHESS.
CLUNK
THE INTELLECTUAL LEVEL, THOUGHT PROCESS, AND PERSONALITY OF ONE'S OPPONENT...
ALL OF THIS CAN BE DETERMINED BY HOW ONE PLAYS CHESS.

I HAVE YET TO LOSE A CHESS MATCH.
DO NOT EXPECT AN EASY VICTORY.

I WOULD NOT HAVE IT ANY OTHER WAY.
GRUDGE FROM BEING CALLED "SMALL"
GRUDGE FROM BEING CALLED "SMALL"

...AH.
THERE'S DUST ON THE CHESS-BOARD...

さっさっさっさっさ、
WIPE WIPE WIPE WIPE WIPE
さっさ
WIPE WIPE
さっさっさっさっさ、
WIPE WIPE WIPE WIPE WIPE
......NH!
?
UNACCEPTABLE...
THIS DUST WON'T COME OFF...
STAAARE
UPON CLOSER EXAMINATION, THERE'S A STAIN AS WELL...
......NGH!
WAIT RIGHT THERE!
I'LL POLISH THIS BOARD UNTIL IT SHINES LIKE A MIRROR, AND THEN OUR CONTEST SHALL BEGIN!
RAAAAH!
SCRUB
SCRUB
SCRUB
だらんぬ
LAZE
COOLED OFF

I SEE THAT PRINCE BRUNO'S CHARACTER IS SOMEWHAT... TIRESOME TO DEAL WITH.
POINTING THIS OUT TO THE PRINCE HIMSELF WOULD LIKELY ONLY HEAP FUEL ON THE FIRE, SO I SHAN'T SPEAK OF IT.
THERE. PERFECT. WHOLLY SATISFACTORY!
CLEANER
SUCH A HASSLE. I'LL MAKE THIS QUICK.
KATAK
!?
EFFORTLESS VICTORY
AGAIN!
TO THE NEXT MATCH!
IT'S TOO SOON TO LET YOUR GUARD DOWN! DON'T YOU WISH TO PROVE YOURSELF!?
OH? THERE'S MORE?
JAB
LAZE
ARE YOU SATISFIED THAT I POSSESS THE PROPER QUALIFICATIONS NOW?
H...
HOW...?
HOW DID I LOSE? I MOVED THIS PIECE HERE, AND THEN...

THIS TUTOR IS CONSID-ERABLY INTELLI-GENT...
N-NO, IT'S TOO SOON TO BE SURE...
I'LL TEST HIM FROM OTHER ANGLES!

MENTAL ARITH-METIC
WHOOOSH

MUSICAL ABILITY

PLAYING CARDS
ROYAL STRAIGHT FLUSH!!
THIS IS FAR BEYOND ORDINARY INTELLECT!

WHAT WILL THE NEXT CHALLENGE BE, THEN?
BUILDING A FIVE-LEVEL CARD TOWER IN THE TIME I SPENT GATHERING MY THOUGHTS...
JUST HOW BROAD A RANGE DO YOU HAVE?
AGAINST ME... ME, WHO HAS HAD NUMEROUS THESES ACCLAIMED BY SCHOLARS WORLDWIDE...
NO! GET AHOLD OF YOURSELF...

MY INTELLECT IS MY PRIDE...!
NO ONE CAN BEST ME IN SHEER ACADEMIC EXPERTISE!!
GRIP

SHWIP
THE NEXT CHALLENGE: YOU'LL BE TAKING A TEST OF MY OWN PERSONAL CREATION!
ARITHMETIC. CHEMISTRY. HISTORY. GEOGRAPHY... ONE HUNDRED CHALLENGING QUESTIONS COMPILED FROM ALL MANNER OF ACADEMIC SUBJECTS.
MOREOVER, EACH QUESTION IS WRITTEN IN ONE OF FIVE RANDOM LANGUAGES!

EVEN YOU WILL FIND YOURSELF STUMPED—
DONE.

BY THE WAY, YOU MADE ONE MISSPELLING IN "FONTAINE" ON QUESTION FIFTY-SEVEN.
I MARKED IT IN RED FOR YOU.
KRINNK
※SOUND OF HIS PRIDE BREAKING INTO LITTLE PIECES

...A PERFECT SCORE. IT'S USELESS. I CAN'T BEST HIM AT ANYTHING...
OVERWHELMING ABILITY... OCCASIONALLY CALLING FORTH INCREDIBLE LUCK...
SO THIS IS WHAT MAKES A TRUE GENIUS...!
FROM AN EARLY AGE, I WAS DETERMINED TO NEVER LOSE TO ANYONE...
I DEVOTED MYSELF TO MY STUDIES SO THAT I WOULD BE SUPERIOR IN EVERYTHING. ACADEMIC SUBJECTS, CULTURE, EVEN MUSIC.
WHAT IN THE WORLD HAVE I—?
NGH!

HMM?
YOU WROTE THIS PIECE?
Y-YES.
I DID...
LET'S SEE. "THE KINGDOM OF GRANZREICH'S FUNDAMENTAL VALUES AS A MODERN NATION"...
HMM. YOU EVEN TOUCH UPON THE EFFECTS OF THE RECENT CONSTRUCTION OF THE RINGSTRASSE ON THE PUBLIC CONSCIOUSNESS... EXCELLENT.
YOU... COULD TELL?
THAT I POURED MY SOUL INTO THAT PARTICULAR POINT...?
YES. AN IMPRESSIVELY IMPARTIAL PERSPECTIVE...NOT THAT OF A ROYAL, BUT OF A SCHOLAR.

HOWEVER, THIS SENTENCE HERE, IN THE PASSAGE REGARDING THE ECONOMIC CRISIS THIRTY YEARS AGO, MAKES IT SOUND AS IF YOU ARE CRITICIZING THE BANKS.
YOU MIGHT CONSIDER REVISING THIS STATEMENT, MAKING YOUR ASSERTION MORE TACTFULLY.

SNATCH

HE MAKES A VALID POINT... IT'S A MINOR PASSAGE, BUT IT FEELS TOO RUSHED...
......

ALSO, YOUR EXAMINATION OF THE HARMONY AMONG COMMONERS DESPITE THEIR VARIOUS ETHNICITIES...
HAD YOU CONSIDERED THAT THE PERFORMANCES OF PUBLIC OPERETTAS AT KARL THEATER MIGHT BE ANOTHER FACTOR?
N-NOW THAT YOU MENTION IT...
IT MAY BE SOMEWHAT OUTSIDE OF YOUR EXPERTISE, BUT YOU'LL FIND THAT TAKING THE ARTS INTO ACCOUNT CAN WIDEN YOUR POINT OF VIEW.

...INCREDIBLE... TO THINK THERE'S SOMEONE IN THIS WORLD WHO COULD DEMONSTRATE SUCH DEEP UNDERSTANDING OF MY WRITING AND OFFER ME SUCH USEFUL GUIDANCE...
HE'S... HE'S...!
SLAM
CLASP

PLEASE, MAY I CALL YOU "MASTER" ...!?
YOU DO REALIZE I AM ONLY A TUTOR...?

F-FORGIVE ME.
I WAS SO OVER-COME WITH DELIGHT THAT I...
FWSH
MASTER, I CAN SAY WITHOUT A DOUBT THAT I HAVE NEVER MET ANYONE MORE WORTHY OF MY RESPECT THAN YOU...
I ADMIT MY DEFEAT ON ALL FRONTS.

PLEASE TAKE ME UNDER YOUR WING!
90°
MAS-TER!!
BACKGROUND: MASTER MASTER MASTER MASTER...
師匠師匠師匠
がばっ
FWIP
UGH.
A MOST DISTURB-ING SHOW OF ATTACH-MENT...

WELL, I SUPPOSE THAT MORE ENTHUSIASM WILL MAKE HIM ALL THE MORE WORTH TEACHING...
PRINCE BRUNO SAID THAT HE WANTED TO TEST ME.
BUT PERHAPS...
...HE WAS ONLY SEARCHING FOR SOMEONE HE COULD GENUINELY LOOK UP TO AS A TEACHER.

STILL... "MASTER" ?
YOU HAVE MUCH TO LEARN, GRASSHOPPER! EN GARDE!
YES, MAS-TER!!!
CHAK
A VERY MASTER-AND-APPRENTICE FEELING...
WHILE I APPRECIATE YOUR ENTHUSIASM, BEING CALLED "MASTER" IS TOO EMBARRASSING.
I WOULD BE GRATEFUL IF YOU ADDRESSED ME AS AN ORDINARY TEACHER.
I AM BUT THE ROYAL TUTOR, AFTER ALL.
AH!

F-FORGIVE MY MIS-STEP...
LET'S SEE...

VERY WELL. IN MY INNER THOUGHTS, I WILL THINK OF YOU AS "MASTER," BUT ALOUD, I WILL ADDRESS YOU AS "PROFES-SOR"!
"PROFESSOR" (READ: "MASTER")
IT'S SETTLED!
PLEASE LET GO OF THIS "MASTER" OBSESSION.

B-BUT I FEEL THAT THE WORD "MASTER" MORE PRECISELY EXPRESSES MY FEELINGS.
IF I WERE TO EXPRESS MY DEEPLY SINCERE DESIRE TO STUDY UNDER YOU AS "X" AND THE STRENGTH OF THE WORD "PROFESSOR" AS "Y"...
FORGIVE ME...BUT I DON'T FOLLOW...
WHAT I MEAN TO SAY, MASTER, IS—
BRU-NIIIE!
BRUNIE!
BAM
LICHT!
!?

I'VE TOLD YOU TIME AND AGAIN TO ALWAYS KNOCK THRICE BEFORE ENTERING MY ROOM!
AWW, WHAT'S THE BIG DEAL? WE'RE BROTHERS!
HOW MANY TIMES DO I HAVE TO TELL YOU!?
THAT CARELESS ATTITUDE OF YOURS IS ABSOLUTELY INEXCUS-ABLE—
NAG NAG
HEY BRUNIE, I'M GONNA BORROW TEACH FOR A BIT!
LIFT
GET BACK HERE! I'M NOT DONE TALKING TO YOU!!
WE BETTER RUUUN!!
YEEEEK—!
WHILE THIS POSITION IS NOT IDEAL...
...TO BE FRANK, I FIND MYSELF GRATEFUL FOR THE OUT.
MAS-TER!
MAS-TER!
I WAS CORRECT... HE'S A TIRESOME ONE...
ぷらーん
DANGLE

THE ROYAL TUTOR

Chapter 4
Interview with a Prince III

THE FIFTH PRINCE, LICHT. FOURTEEN YEARS OF AGE.
WITH HIS HANDSOME FACE AND BRIGHT PERSONALITY, HE EASILY ESTABLISHES INTIMACY WITH ROYALS FROM OTHER KINGDOMS.
HE IS KNOWN TO SNEAK INTO THE CITY FREQUENTLY AND ENJOYS MARKED POPULARITY AMONG THE POPULACE, PARTICULARLY AMONG WOMEN.
ACCORDING TO MY NOTES, THIS SUMS UP HIS CHARACTER.
......
THIS DOESN'T BOTHER ME AS SUCH, BUT...THE BLOOD HAS GONE TO MY HEAD.
STILL STUCK UPSIDE DOWN

TEACH! YOU'RE INVITED TO MY ROOM!
URP!
I TAKE IT BACK. I REALLY SHOULD HAVE A WORD WITH HIM.
AHEM. YOUR HIGHNESS, CARRYING YOUR TEACHER IN SUCH A WAY IS HIGHLY—
LADIIIES! HE'S ALL YOOOURS!
OOOH!
HE'S THE CHILD TEACHER YOUR HIGHNESS TOLD US ABOUT!?
HE'S SOOOOO CUUUTE!
OOH, I JUST WANNA SNUGGLE-WUGGLE HIM!
THIS CHILDISH APPEARANCE OCCASIONALLY HAS ITS ADVANTAGES.
OH DEAR. WHAT WAS I SAYING?
I SUPPOSE I'LL PUT THE LECTURE ASIDE FOR THE TIME BEING.

SORRY TO SNATCH YOU UP LIKE THAT!
IT'S JUST THAT, ONCE I MENTIONED YOU, EVERY-BODY WAS GIDDY TO MEET YOU.
WHO ARE THESE YOUNG LADIES...?
MY FRIENDS!
WHAAAT? JUST FRIENDS?
POUT
POUT
HMPH! IF YOU'RE GOING TO BE SO COLD, MAYBE WE SHOULD SHOW OURSELVES BACK TO THE CITY!
SQUEEZE
"JUST" FRIENDS? I THOUGHT YOU KNEW THAT YOU'RE VERY SPECIAL FRIENDS TO ME...
DON'T GO...
LOVE ME MORE...
AAHN!
EEE!
SOOO CUTE!
I'LL LOVE YOU SO BAD, PRINCE!
... "FRIENDS" ...?

I SEE. WHERE MY MATERIALS MENTION THAT PRINCE LICHT FREQUENTLY SNEAKS INTO THE CITY...
...THE SUBTEXT IS THAT HE FREQUENTLY ABSCONDS TO CONSORT WITH WOMEN-FOLK.
APPALLING.
I REQUIRE A PRIVATE AUDIENCE WITH PRINCE LICHT.
WOULD YOU BE SO KIND AS TO EXCUSE YOURSELVES FOR THE TIME BEING?
AWWW, HEINEEE! HOW COLD!

SORRY, DO YOU MIND?
IF YOUR HIGHNESS SAYS SO...

MY GOODNESS.
PRINCE LICHT IS ACTUALLY COOPERATIVE, UNLIKE THE FIRST TWO PRINCES.
MY APOLOGIES...
...FOR INTERRUPTING YOUR FUN.
...NAH.

I DON'T MIND.
ACTUALLY, THERE'S SOMETHING I WANTED TO DISCUSS WITH YOU IN PRIVATE ANYWAY.
......!
IT COULDN'T BE...
YOU LOOK LIKE A CHILD, BUT YOU'RE A GROWN-UP, RIGHT?
SO...HOW GROWN ARE YOU DOWN THERE...?
STARE
WHAM
AUGH!!!

WHA...!? TEACH!
YOU'RE A TEACHER! YOU CAN'T KICK A STUDENT IN THE FACE!!
YOU GOBLIN!
MERELY EDUCA-TIONAL REIN-FORCE-MENT.
WHAT'S YOUR PROBLEM? IT WAS AN INNOCENT QUESTION!
BOO! BOO!
"INNO-CENT" HOW, PRAY TELL?
THAT WAS BLATANTLY INAPPROPRIATE.

HERE.
NOW TAKE THIS TEST TO GAUGE YOUR ACADEMIC LEVEL.
THWACK
HUH? AREN'T YOU BEING TOO CURT WITH ME ALL OF A SUDDEN?
I AM A PRINCE AND ALL...

A TEST, HUUUH...?
DO I HAVE TO TAKE THIS? BOOORING...

BORING, BORING...
BORED.
BING
HEY LADIES, DO YOU KNOW THE ANSWER TO THIS ONE?
HMM? WHAT IS IT?
WHY ARE YOU TURNING THIS INTO A GROUP ACTIVITY?
FINISH IT YOURSELF.

YEESH, YOU'RE SO PICKY.
WELL, WHATEVER MAKES YOU HAPPY...
SIIIGH.
HOW PATRON-IZING.

OH YEAH! DID YOU TALK TO LEONIE AND BRUNIE?
YAK
YAK
TOTAL WEIRDOS, AREN'T THEY? LEONIE IS ALL MUSCLE, NO BRAIN.
YAK

OH! OH! LISTEN TO THIS! THE OTHER DAY, LEONIE—IT WAS A DAY WE HAD AN IMPORTANT DINNER PARTY—GUESS WHAT HE DID!
YAK
YAK
BRUNIE WAS EXPLAINING THIS COMPLICATED THESIS, AND LEONIE CON-CENTRATED SO HARD THAT HE LITERALLY GOT A FEVER—
YAK
PRINCE.
PLEASE STOP CHATTING AND FINISH YOUR TEST.

BUT I'M ALREADY DONE!
YAY!
GOOD HEAVENS.

WHY, ONCE YOU SAW FIT TO PUT YOUR PEN TO PAPER, YOU FINISHED IT IN THE BLINK OF AN EYE.
UH-HUH! PEOPLE TELL ME I CAN DO ANYTHING I PUT MY MIND TO!
THEN PLEASE PUT YOUR MIND TO THE TASK FROM THE START. HONESTLY, I WOULD LIKE MY WASTED TIME RETURNED TO ME.
IF YOU'LL EXCUSE ME, I MUST GO SEE THE REMAINING PRINCE.
OUCH...
KLAK

AH! WAIT! WAIT!
I HAVE A QUES-TION!
YANK

YOU MAY ASK IT, PROVIDED YOU UNDER-STAND I SHALL NOT ANSWER YOUR PREVIOUS QUESTION.
ZWOOSH
OOH. I STILL DO WANNA KNOW THAT...BUT THIS IS ABOUT SOMETHING ELSE.
TO BE BLUNT, WHAT ARE YOU?
......
WHAT DO YOU MEAN BY THAT?

ALL OUR OLD TUTORS WERE UNIVERSITY PROFESSORS AND WHATNOT. FAMOUS PEOPLE WITH PROPER TITLES.
THAT'S A GIVEN, SINCE THEY WERE CALLED TO WORK FOR THE ROYAL FAMILY.
BUT I'VE NEVER HEARD OF A HEINE WITTGEN-STEIN.
I HAVE TO WONDER IF YOU'RE FATHER'S PERSONAL MEDIATOR...
A SHARP STARE... AS THOUGH IT MIGHT PENETRATE MY VERY SOUL...

EH, NOT THAT I WOULD KNOW THE NAMES OF ANY PROFESSORS.
AH-HA-HA, SORRIES! I BET YOU'RE ANOTHER FAMOUS SCHOLAR WHO WON SOME AWARD OR SOME SUCH, RIGHT?
THAT STUFF BORES ME TO TEARS. I DON'T KEEP UP WITH ANY OF IT. MY BAD!
......

PRINCEY-POO? ALL DONE?
OH DEAR, WHAT'S GOTTEN INTO YOU?
YOU LOOK SO SERI-OUS!
...IT'S NOTH-ING.
WE WERE IN THE MIDDLE OF A SERIOUS DIALOGUE.
WEREN'T WE, TEACH?
HE WANTED TO KNOW ABOUT THIS AND THAT. ♡
YOU KNOOOW, ADULT PROBLEMS. ♡
OWIE!
WHACK
EDUCA-TIONAL REIN-FORCE-MENT!!
EEEE!
EEEE!

SEE YOU LATER, TEACH!
EXCUSE ME.
BYE-BYE, HEINE CUTIE! ♡
IT FEELS ALMOST AS THOUGH HE WAS DANCING ME ABOUT IN THE PALM OF HIS HAND...
...HMM...

THE YOUNGEST OF THE BROTHERS, EH?
UNDERESTI-MATING HIM BASED ON HIS AGE COULD PROVE TO BE A GRAVE MISSTEP.

NOW, THEN. I SHOULD TAKE A MOMENT TO COMPOSE MYSELF.
FLIP
MY FINAL INTERVIEW IS WITH PRINCE KAI.
KNOCK
KNOCK
SILENCE
......
OH!
PARDON ME, BUT PRINCE KAI DOES NOT SEEM TO BE IN HIS ROOM. DO YOU KNOW WHERE HE MIGHT BE?
I'M AFRAID WE HAVEN'T SEEN HIM.

I'VE CUT IT CLOSE. ONLY ONE MORE HOUR UNTIL THE CLOCK STRIKES FOUR, WHEN I HAVE MY APPOINTMENT WITH THE PRINCES.
TMP
I NEED TO FIND PRINCE KAI—AND QUICKLY!

THE ROYAL TUTOR

Chapter 5
Interview with a Prince IV

I MUST MAKE HASTE...
PUNCTUALITY IS THE MOST ELEMENTARY STEP TOWARD BUILDING TRUST.
WHIRL

HMM?
HAFF!
HAFF!
カぷっ
CHOMP
OH DEAR.
A PET KEPT HERE IN THE PALACE, PER-HAPS?
I BESEECH YOU—RETURN MY NOTES, DOG!
ガッ
TRIP

!!?
A CORPSE ...!?
IN THE PALACE COURTYARD...?
HAFF! HFF!
ZZZ...
NO...THE BOY IS MERELY ASLEEP.
FLIP

THE SECOND PRINCE, KAI. SEVEN-TEEN YEARS OF AGE.
A TACITURN BOY WHO RARELY APPEARS BEFORE THE PUBLIC.
HE WAS SUSPENDED FROM MILITARY ACADEMY AFTER A VIOLENT OUTBURST AND IS INFAMOUS FOR HIS FEROCIOUS DISPOSITION.
I'VE FOUND HIM. PRINCE KAI.
THE MOST DANGEROUS OF THE PRINCES...!

THE GLARE HE TURNED AT ME EARLIER— A HINT OF HOSTILITY LURKED IN THOSE EYES...
NOW, THEN. HOW SHALL I APPROACH HIM?
......
GLARE
FWOOSH
!

GRAB
YANK
...NH!
...KNH...!

ふにっ
RUB

......
ふにふにふに
PET
PET
PET
PET
PET
PET
......

...OOPS.
DROP
ぱっ

PET
PET
PET
PET
PET
"OOPS" ...?
HE MISTOOK ME FOR THE DOG ...?

...NEW...
...TEACHER...
HE ALREADY CONSIDERS ME HIS TEACHER, DOES HE?
PERHAPS I CAN BE STRAIGHT-FORWARD WITH HIM.
GOOD DAY, YOUR HIGHNESS. TAKING AN AFTERNOON NAP, ARE WE?

THIS IS...
...MY FAVORITE PLACE TO NAP...
YES, IT IS CALM AND QUIET. AN EXCELLENT CHOICE.

SOME-TIMES... EVERY-THING TIRES ME...
THAT'S WHEN...
...I SLEEP HERE...
A PRINCE'S STATION BRINGS WITH IT MUCH PRESSURE, I'M SURE.
THIS IS ESPECIALLY TRUE FOR PRINCE KAI, THE ELDEST PRINCE IN THE PALACE WHILE HIS OLDER BROTHER IS AWAY...

TOO TIRED TO TALK...
TOO TIRED TO DRESS...

TOO TIRED TO BREATHE...
...YOU'VE DONE WELL TO SURVIVE THIS LONG, THEN...

......

AH...BUT... I LOVE TO EAT...
TWINKLE
ぱぁ
I DIDN'T ASK...

THE NOTES I GATHERED ON HIM COULD NOT HAVE BEEN MORE INACCURATE. HE SEEMS TO BE A RATHER CALM, UNHURRIED PRINCE…

HOW, THEN, DID HE GARNER SUCH A FEARFUL REPUTATION?

!
GLARE

TEACHER … THAT CLOUD…
…LOOKS LIKE AN APPLE…
YUM.
…S…
SO IT DOES…
……
AHEM…
…DID YOU NOT JUST GLARE AT ME…?
?
?

PRINCE, IF I MAY WAGER A GUESS, DO YOUR SHARP EYES...
...HAPPEN TO LEAVE OTHERS WITH THE IMPRESSION THAT YOU ARE GLARING AT THEM, WHEN YOU ARE SIMPLY WEARING AN ORDINARY EXPRESSION?

...ALL THE TIME.
AHA. DO YOU NOT CORRECT THEM?
CAN'T CHANGE MY EYES... AND...I SPEAK SLOW...
BAD FIRST IMPRES-SIONS... PROBABLY... TOO LATE... TO CHANGE...
YOUR HIGH-NESS...

I MUST ASK—WHY HAVE YOU BEEN PETTING MY HAND?
PET
PET
LOVES CUTE THINGS

IN THAT CASE, IS IT SAFE TO ASSUME THAT YOU NEVER GLARED AT ME...
...AND HOLD NO HOSTILITY TOWARD ME?
ふに PET
I'M... HAPPY... TO HAVE A NEW TEACHER...
YOU'RE... THE FIRST TEACHER...
...TO TALK TO ME...
THANK YOU...
PRINCE KAI...
TEACHER... IS THAT... A TEST...?
FOR ME...?
AH. YES, IT IS.

PLEASE COMPLETE IT.
SKRICH SKRICH
TEACHER... ME...AND MY BROTHERS... ARE IN YOUR HANDS...
PLEASED TO MEET YOU...
THE PLEA-SURE IS ALL MINE.
IF YOU'LL EXCUSE ME.
NOD
PRINCE KAI...AS EXPECTED OF THE SECOND SON...
...IS A MATURE, GENTLE FELLOW.

AND HERE I EXPECTED HIM TO BE THE MOST UNMANAGE-ABLE OF THE BROTHERS...
"YOU'RE... THE FIRST TEACHER...TO TALK TO ME... THANK YOU..."
......

INTELLIGENCE GATHERED BY A THIRD PARTY SIMPLY CANNOT BE RELIED UPON.
RRRIP
I'LL HAVE TO PEN MY OWN NOTES FROM SCRATCH.
HE RE-EVALUATED HIS DUTIES AS THE ROYAL TUTOR WITH A RENEWED VIGOR.

THE ROYAL TUTOR

Chapter 6
You Needn't Welcome Me

TAP
TAP

THERE. I'VE FINISHED GRADING THE PRINCES' TESTS...

ALMOST TIME FOR OUR APPOINT-MENT.

BUT WILL EACH OF THEM MAKE AN APPEAR-ANCE?
Kai
Bruno
Leonhard
Licht

GONG
GONG
KNOCK
KNOCK

KACHAK
I AM AT YOUR DISPOSAL, MASTER!
FWIP
WELL, I HAD NO DOUBT THAT YOU WOULD BE FIRST TO ARRIVE...
90°

PRAY, COULD YOU STOP ADDRESSING ME AS "MASTER"?
PARTICULARLY IN FRONT OF YOUR BROTHERS.
IT'S... UNCOMFORTABLE...
M-MY MISTAKE!

"P-PROFESSOR," THEN...?
BADUM
BADUM
THAT WILL DO.
WHY THE POUNDING HEART...?

KACHAK

HULLO, TEACH! ♪
TA-DAA!
... TEACHER... I'M... HERE...
GOOD DAY.
GUH!
YOU TWO! WHY IS IT...
...YOU FAIL TO ADDRESS THE PROFESSOR WITH THE PROPER FORMALITY!?
GEEZ, WHO CARES? YOU'RE TOO UPTIGHT, BRUNIE!
MAS— THE PRO-FESSOR DESERVES YOUR RESPECT!
MAS—THE PROFESSOR MAY NOT SCOLD YOU, BUT IT STILL HOLDS TRUE!
WHY DO YOU KEEP SAYING "MASS," BRUNIE?
?

IT'S COOL, RIGHT, TEACH?
WE'RE BEST BUDS AND ALL, NO?
WHA ...!?
YAY!
WHEN THE HELL DID YOU GET SO...?
HOW INEXCUSABLY IMPOLITE... AND ENVIABLE, SO ENVIABLE ...
I'M JEALOUS !!
TCH.
PLEASE CALM DOWN.
YOU MAY SPEAK TO ME HOWEVER YOU LIKE.
YOUR HIGHNESSES, AFTER ALL, HOLD A FAR HIGHER STATION THAN I.
AH. COULD I ASK YOU NOT TO PUT YOUR HAND ON MY SHOULDER?
IT IS MY PERSONAL BELIEF AND MY PHILOSOPHY AS A TEACHER THAT THE RELATIONSHIP BETWEEN TEACHER AND STUDENT SHOULD BE BUILT ON A FOUNDATION OF TRUST...
AH. WOULD YOU MIND GIVING ME A LITTLE MORE SPACE?
YOU'RE TOO CLOSE.
WH—? HEY! YOU'RE BEING COLD TO ME!!

IT'S YOUR JUST DESERTS FOR YOUR LACK OF MANNERS.
GOOD GRIEF. YOU'RE ALWAYS SO UNSEEMLY...
I'M JUST UNSEEMLY ENOUGH, THANK YOU!
YOUR UNSEEMLINESS IS UNBEARABLE! EVERY DAY YOU BRING A NEW STRANGE WOMAN TO YOUR ROOM!
HMPH! LIKE YOU'RE ONE TO TALK!
BLEEH.
I MEAN, SERIOUSLY!? YOU SURE YOU'RE NOT JEALOUS OF YOUR KID BROTHER JUST 'COS YOU CAN'T GET A GIRL, EGGHEAD?
TCH. I CAN'T BELIEVE I'M STUCK WITH THIS HARD-HEADED NITPICKER FOR A BROTHER!
I BEG YOUR PARDON? WELL, I WOULD PREFER NOT TO HAVE A YOUNGER BROTHER WHO IS ROTTEN TO HIS VERY CORE!
GRR! SIT DOWN AND I'LL BEAT THE ROT OUT OF YOU!
I'M NOT GONNA BE LECTURED BY SOMEONE AS SNOBBY AS YOU!
SILENT
ちょこーん
HMM.
SHALL I INTERVENE?
SWOOP
PRINCE KAI.

GLARE
!
JOLT
HAAH...
BE...
DUN-DUN
...NICE...!

BRUNO... LICHT...
...BE NICE...!
I LOST MY TEMPER... I APOLOGIZE, BROTHER...
SORRY, KAINIE...
THEY STOPPED.

YOU MAKE A MOST EFFECTIVE INTERMEDIARY, PRINCE KAI.
WELL, YOU ARE THE OLDEST HERE.
...LOVE ALL OF MY BROTH-ERS...
...BEST WHEN ALL GET ALONG...
HE'S SO PURE-HEARTED, YOU CAN'T ARGUE WITH HIM.
ぱちぱち
CLAP CLAP

...WITH TEACHER... TOO...
WHY, I'M HONORED.
...NOW, THEN. THE ONLY ABSENT BROTHER IS PRINCE LEON-HARD.
WILL HE COME ...?

MEAN-WHILE, LEON-HARD...
DID ALL OF MY BROTHERS FINISH THEIR INTERVIEWS WITH THAT PIP-SQUEAK OF A TEACHER?
...NONE OF THE OTHER TUTORS WERE ABLE TO CATCH ME WHEN I RAN FROM LESSONS.
NOT ONLY THAT, BUT THEY NEVER HAD ANYTHING TO TEACH DEAREST BROTHER BRUNO. HE WAS ALREADY TOO SUPERIOR.
NOR COULD THEY MOTIVATE LICHT...
...OR EVEN SO MUCH AS SPEAK TO DEAR BROTHER KAI.
IN THE END, THEY ALL RETREATED.

THAT INSOLENT HEINE WILL BE CRUSHED BY THE WEIGHT OF HIS OWN POWERLESSNESS BY NOW...
MAYBE I'LL HAVE MYSELF A LOOK AT HIS CRYING FACE.
CREAK
AH-HA-HA-HA-HA!
HEH-HEH-HEH-HEH...
NGAH!
BAM
LEON-HARD!?
YOU ARE LATE, PRINCE LEONHARD.

WH-WHY ARE YOU LAUGHING IT UP WITH A TEACHER!?
MERE HOURS AGO YOU WERE ON MY SIDE! WE AGREED TO OUST HIM! TRAITOR!
TRAITOR? OH, LEONIE...
ACTUALLY, I'VE TAKEN A LIKING TO HIM!
ME TOO...
WH—?
LICHT! ELDER BROTHER!
WHAT IN THE BLAZES...?
HAVING HIM AROUND WILL KEEP THE LADIES HAPPY.
EEE!
SO CUTE!
SOOO CUTE!
ULTERIOR MOTIVES
TEACHER... SMALL... CUTE... PET...
ふに PET
ふに PET
ULTERIOR MOTIVES HERE TOO

N-NO...HOW DID HE WIN BOTH OF THEM OVER SO QUICKLY?
STAGGER
H-HE'S BRAIN-WASHED THEM!
GRIT
I WON'T BE FOOLED!
BRUNO, MY BROTH-ER!
HE CAN'T HAVE BRAIN-WASHED YOU, YES!?
WHIRL
PRO-FESSOR HEINE IS A TRULY EXCELLENT TUTOR, YET HE COULD NOT BE MORE HUMBLE. A MAN OF EXEMPLARY CHARACTER. SUCH IS THE MARK OF A TRUE GENIUS...
...
BROTHER!!
THE MOST HOPE-LESSLY AFFLICTED

NOW, THEN, AS YOU ARE ALL GATHERED...
...I'LL RETURN YOUR TESTS FROM TODAY.
HUH!?

TH-THAT'S NOT WHAT I CAME HERE FOR.
I'M LEAV-ING!
HOLD ON, LEONIE.
YOU ALREADY TOOK THE TEST. MAY AS WELL FIND OUT YOUR GRADE!
WH—
GRAB
IT'S A CONTEST— YOU VERSUS ME!
UNHAND ME, LICHT, YOU FOOL!
AHEM. TO BEGIN...

BRUNO, THE THIRD SON: ONE HUNDRED POINTS
100
NATURALLY.
BLEEEH.
FREAK.

KAI, THE SECOND SON: EIGHTY-SEVEN POINTS
WHOA! THAT'S GOOD!
...AVER-AGE.
WHY ARE YOU SURPRISED? BROTHER HAS ALWAYS GOTTEN GOOD MARKS.
LICHT, THE FIFTH SON: SIXTY POINTS.
YOWCH! AND THESE WERE BASIC QUESTIONS... I'M BEHIND...

LEONHARD, THE FOURTH SON: ONE POINT
....
......
......
FWIP
ふいっ
......

TH-THAT'S IMPOSSIBLY LOW...
EVEN WITH AN AVERSION TO ACADEMICS ...
I'M SURE THIS IS SOME KIND OF MISTAKE. LET ME SEE IT.
DID YOU FILL IN THE ANSWER SHEET WITH YOUR ANSWERS OFF BY ONE...?
......

!?

HE ANSWERED EVERY QUESTION IN THE RIGHT PLACE, YET EVERY SINGLE ONE OF HIS ANSWERS IS INCORRECT...
Leonhard
HIS LONE POINT IS A PITY POINT FOR WRITING HIS NAME...!
AH-HA-HA-HA! LEONIE, FOR REAL!?
I'M... ERR... SORRY...
SSK
KYEH HEH HEH!
THIS IS WHY I DIDN'T WANT TO TAKE ANY TESTS...
URGH...

H...
HOW CAN I ENCOURAGE HIM?
I'LL SHUT THIS ONE UP FOR NOW, AT LEAST, BUT...
MMH! MMFH!
DON'T NEED TO BE UPSET... YOU'RE A GOOD BOY...
ATHLETICS... ARE YOUR FORTE...
PAT
THANK YOU, BROTHER!

Y-YEAH, THAT'S RIGHT...! I'LL BE OKAY...
...AS LONG AS I MAKE UP FOR IT ELSEWHERE...!

BLUNT
STILL, THIS SCORE IS SIMPLY DREADFUL, PRINCE LEONHARD.
SHOCK
HOWEVER, YOU...
...HMM?
TRMBL
TRMBL
TRMBL

I-I'VE NEVER BEEN SO HUMILIATED... THIS IS ALL BECAUSE YOU FORCED ME TO TAKE THAT STUPID TEST!
I...
I...
I KNEW TEACHERS WERE THE ENEMY!!
AH.
DASH
LEON-HARD!
LEO-NIE!

GAH! TOO FAST!
ZOOM
WOOOW. NOBODY CAN CATCH UP TO LEONIE WHEN HE RUNS FULL TILT.
YEAH...HE WON'T BE BACK FOR A WHILE.
....

I BEG YOUR PARDON FOR MY YOUNGER BROTHER'S RUDENESS.
...NO, IT IS I WHO SHOULD APOLO-GIZE.
LEON-HARD...
...DESPISES THE VERY NOTION OF TEACHERS.

OUR FIRST TUTOR WAS EXCEPTIONALLY STRICT.
AS LEONHARD WAS NEVER ACADEMICALLY INCLINED, HE IN PARTICULAR WAS AT THE MERCY OF THE TUTOR'S ROD.
HE HAS REVILED ALL MANNER OF EDUCATORS EVER SINCE.
IT'S NOT THAT HE THINKS ILL OF YOU IN PARTICULAR—
IN THAT CASE...
...I'LL HAVE TO TEACH HIM.
WHA...?

I AM HIS TUTOR.
I'LL BE THE ONE TO TEACH HIM...
...THAT TEACHERS ARE NOT THE ENEMY.

CREAK
TMP
!
LEAP
N-NO WAY! WE'RE THREE FLOORS UP!
PRO-FES-SOR...
PROFES-SOR!
MASTERRR!!
U-UH... "MASTER" ...?
SHIVER
A MOMENT OF ALARM FOR ALL THOSE PRESENT

CLOP
CLOP
CLOP
CLOP
WHEN I'M MOVING, I CAN GET AWAY FROM THE BAD THINGS...
PRINCE.
PRINCE LEONHARD!
WHY CAN'T YOU UNDERSTAND SUCH A SIMPLE QUESTION?

WHERE DO YOU THINK YOU'RE GOING?
COME BACK HERE!
PRINCE!!

I'M ALWAYS RUNNING.
EVEN THOUGH I KNOW I SHOULDN'T.
I THINK I ALWAYS HAVE BEEN, EVER SINCE BACK THEN—
SQUEEZE
PRINCE.
PRINCE LEONHARD.

RRRRUMBLE
RRRRUMBLE

UWAAAH!!
THAT RIDING TECHNIQUE...
IT'S LUDICROUS...!!

I AM SORRY THAT YOU MUST SEE ME IN SUCH AN IMPROPER RIDING POSTURE.
YOU SEE, AS MY LEGS ARE TOO SHORT, THIS WAS THE ONLY WAY I COULD RIDE. I DO HOPE YOU'LL EXCUSE IT.
RUMBLE
RUMBLE
RRRRUMBLE
WOULD YOU BE SO KIND AS TO HALT YOUR HORSE?
I WISH TO SPEAK WITH YOU.
——NH!!
——GH!!
NO ONE RIDES LIKE THAT!
YOU'RE SCARING ME! STAY AWAY! IDIOT!!
IF YOU REFUSE TO STOP, YOU LEAVE ME WITH NO CHOICE.
THIS WILL BE A BIT ROUGH...

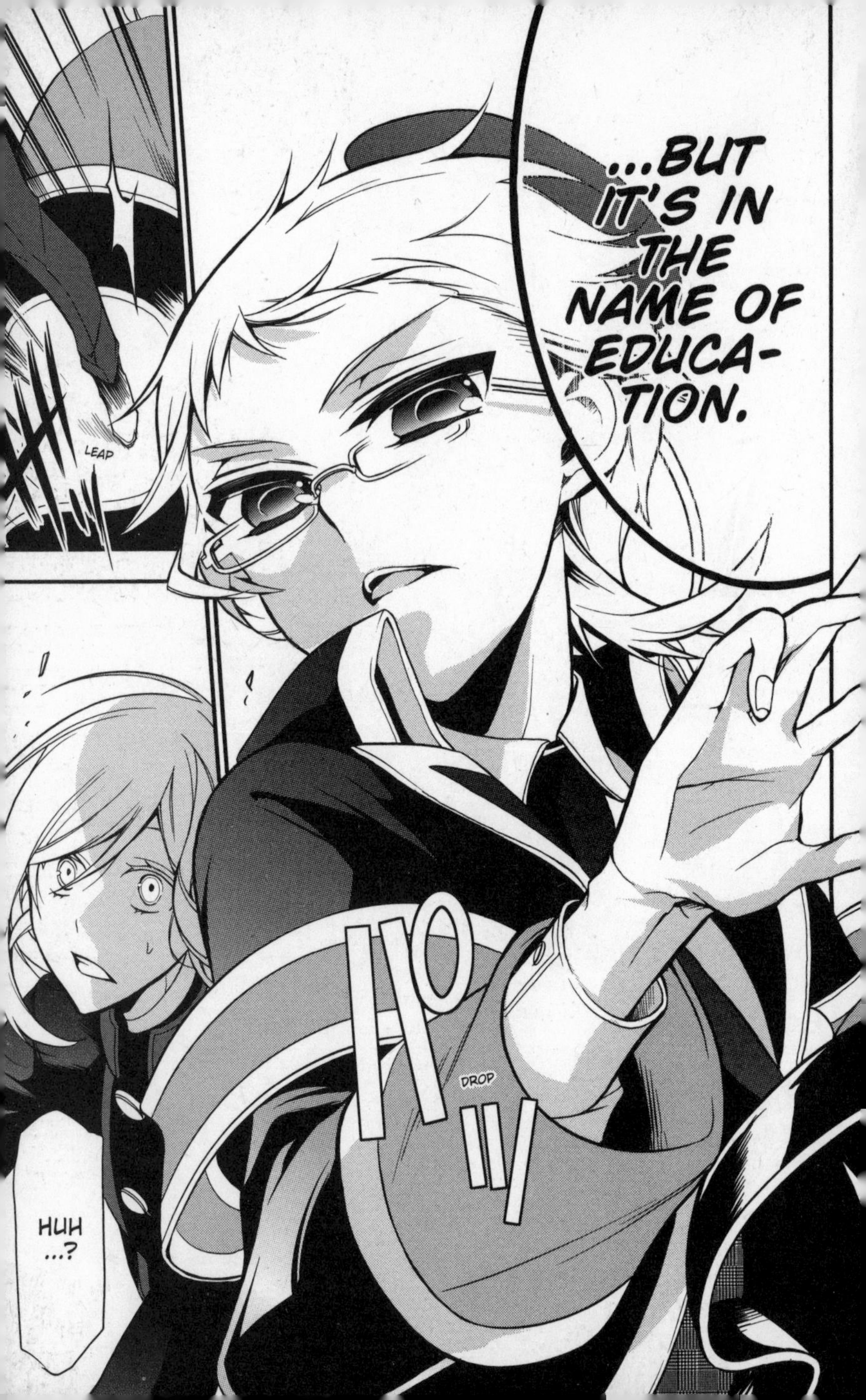
...BUT IT'S IN THE NAME OF EDUCA-TION.
LEAP
DROP
HUH ...?

WAUGH!!
WHUMP

CLOP
CLOP
CLOP
CLOP

RUSTLE
むくっ
I APOLOGIZE FOR RESORTING TO EXTREME MEASURES.
HOWEVER, THE SOONER ONE CORRECTS A MISUNDERSTANDING, THE BETTER, IN MY OPINION.

GIVEN THE SPEED OF OUR HORSES, THE ANGLE OF DESCENT...
...AND WHICH FLORA WOULD PROVIDE THE MOST CUSHIONING...
...I CALCULATED THE SAFEST TIMING TO ACT.

PAT
PAT
AS SUCH, I BELIEVE YOU ARE UNHURT...

TWITCH
ぱく
TWITCH
ぱく
OH DEAR.

M-MADNESS... IT'S NOT POSSIBLE ...
NOT WITH THAT ABSURD RIDING POSTURE...
SLIDE
WHAT THE DEVIL ARE YOU!?
NONE OF THE OTHER TUTORS EVER CAME CLOSE TO CATCHING UP TO ME...!

...I'M NOT AT LIBERTY TO DISCUSS MY BACK-GROUND.
HOW-EVER...
TMP
...IF IT PLEASES YOU...
...SHALL I TELL YOU WHY I WAS ABLE TO CATCH UP WITH YOU?

I DO NOT INTEND TO BLAME YOU AT ALL FOR HAVING NO INCLINATION FOR ACADEMICS.
B-BUT YOU SAID MY SCORE WAS DREADFUL...
......!
THAT IS BECAUSE I...
...AM CUT FROM A DIFFERENT CLOTH THAN ANY OF THE TUTORS YOU'VE HAD BEFORE.

CHANGING THAT IS A TEACHER'S JOB, IS IT NOT?

MORE-OVER, MY TUTORING DOES NOT END AT ACADEMIC SUB-JECTS.
IT ALSO EXTENDS TO MANNERS, SOCIAL SKILLS, AND SO ON.
YOU WILL ATTEND LESSONS TAILORED TO EACH OF THESE AREAS, WITH THE GOAL OF BECOMING A WORTHY CANDI-DATE FOR THE CROWN.

THUS, THERE IS NO NEED TO BE DIS-COURAGED OVER ONE BAD MARK.
I WAS ABOUT TO EXPLAIN THIS...
...WHEN YOU TOOK OFF.
....

SHP
YOU DO NOT NEED TO WELCOME ME AS ROYAL TUTOR.
HOWEVER, I AM THE ONLY TEACHER WHO CAN CATCH YOU.
HOW DOES THIS SOUND TO YOU?

IF YOU WANT TO STOP RUNNING AWAY...
...WILL YOU NOT TAKE MY HAND AND GIVE IT YOUR BEST SHOT?

......

ちょこん
PINCH

....
WHAT'S THIS, THEN?
....

YOUR TROPHY FOR CATCHING UP TO ME.
...THIS MUCH.

I SUPPOSE I CAN TRY...
...THIS MUCH.

...VERY WELL.
I AM AT YOUR SERVICE, YOUR HIGHNESS.
......

A...
SNATCH
ANYWAY, THE SUN IS ABOUT TO SET!

I'M GOING BACK.
MY BROTHERS AND GRAND-MOTHER WILL BE WORRIED.
YES, YOUR HIGH-NESS.

...HMM? WHERE ARE WE?
WHILE WE ARE STILL WITHIN THE PALACE GROUNDS...
...THEY ARE SO VAST THAT WE COULD NOT MAKE OUR WAY HOME BEFORE DARK ON FOOT.

PATRIZIA, WHERE HAVE YOU GONE? RETURN TO ME!
FWEET

......
HEY.
THE HORSES AREN'T COMING BACK.

......
......

......
WHY...

WHY AM I STUCK SPENDING THE NIGHT CAMPING OUT!? I'M A PRINCE...!
BECAUSE YOU GALLOPED SO FAR AWAY.
HERE, I ROASTED SOME NUTS.
YOU'RE THE ONE WHO LET THE HORSES RUN OFF!!
I TAKE IT BACK! I DON'T NEED A TUTOR!
GET OUT!
"GET OUT"? I CAN'T BE ANY MORE OUTSIDE THAN THIS.
SHUT UP!
MEAN-WHILE, AT THE PALACE ...
MASTER!! LEON-HARD!!
Y-YOUR HIGHNESS, PLEASE WAIT! THE ROYAL GUARD WILL CONDUCT A SEARCH!
EH, THEY'LL BE BACK IN THE MORNING.
'COS THEY LIVE HERE AND ALL!
NOD
AAAAAH!

KNOCK
KNOCK
GOOD MORNING, HERR WITTGEN-STEIN.
IT IS TIME TO RISE FOR THE DAY.
ガチャッ
KACHAK

しん
SILENCE
HMM ...? HERR WITTGEN-STEIN...?

みっちり
SQUOOSH
SIR!!

Chapter 7
The Princes' Secret!?

GOOD MORNING, HERR WITTGEN-STEIN! ♡
TEE-HEE! THERE GOES THE LITTLEST TUTOR...
I HEARD HE ROLLED INTO THE SPACE BETWEEN HIS BED AND THE WALL! ♡
HOW ADOR-ABLE! ♡
GOOD MORNING.
ALTHOUGH YESTERDAY WAS BUT THE FIRST DAY OF MY TENURE AS ROYAL TUTOR...
...IT WAS QUITE THE EVENTFUL ONE.
PRINCE LEONHARD AND I WERE LOST IN THE PALACE GARDENS.
THANKFULLY, WE WERE RESCUED SAFE AND SOUND, AND NOTHING CAME OF IT.

THIS IS YOUR ROOM, HERR WITTGENSTEIN.
MAKE YOURSELF AT HOME.
A MARVELOUS ROOM FOR A COMMONER LIKE MYSELF.
THANK YOU.

キラキラ
TWINKLE
TWINKLE
ふかふか
SOFT
SOFT
......
ごろごろー ごろごろー
ROLL
ROLL
ROLL
ROLL
CAN'T GET COMFORT-ABLE...
スポッ
SHOONK
AH.

THIS MORN-ING
EEK!
みっちり
SQUISH
UNABLE TO ESCAPE MY TINY PRISON BY MY OWN POWER...
...I DIDN'T GET A WINK OF SLEEP.

AS A LIVE-IN TUTOR, I'LL HAVE TO ADAPT TO THE ROYAL LIFESTYLE.
GROGGY GROGGY
しょぼしょぼ
NOW THEN, TODAY'S SCHEDULE... PRINCE LEONHARD, PRINCE BRUNO, PRINCE LICHT, PRINCE KAI.
I PLANNED THEIR LESSONS IN THE SAME ORDER AS YESTERDAY'S INTERVIEWS.

"I SUPPOSE I CAN TRY THIS MUCH"...
PINCH
GIVEN WHAT HE SAID...
...EVEN PRINCE LEONHARD SHOULD PUT A BIT OF EFFORT INTO HIS STUDIES.

YES-TER-DAY
NOOO! I'LL NEVER STUDY!
OUTTA MY WAY!
......
NOW, WHAT SHALL I DO IF HE'S ALREADY RUN OFF?
KACHAK
FORGIVE MY INTRUSION, YOUR HIGHNESS.

I'M READY FOR MY LESSONS ...
...HEINE.
POP
ポンッ
WH— WHAT'S WITH THAT REACTION?
YOUR HAT...
EXCUSE ME.
I'M A BIT SURPRISED TO SEE THAT YOUR HIGHNESS DID NOT RUN FROM LESSONS.

I-IT'S NOT LIKE I WANT TO STUDY OR ANY-THING!
AND I'M STILL NOT ACCEPTING YOU AS MY TUTOR EITHER!
B—
BUT I SAID I WOULD TRY. SO I WILL.
...FOR NOW.
PRINCE LEONHARD...

THEN LET'S THROW OURSELVES INTO YOUR STUDIES, SHALL WE?
WE'LL BEGIN WITH BASIC SUMS.
BAM
O-OKAY!
THREE MIN-UTES LATER
ふにゃー
SNOOOOZE
ZZ

YOUR HIGHNESS. PRINCE LEONHARD.
HWHA ...?
......
OH, IT'S JUST A DEER...
GOOD NIGHT.
WHOM ARE YOU CALLING A DEER?
PLEASE DO NOT FALL ASLEEP.
D-DRAT! I DOZED OFF...
BOLT
HRMPH.
IT WOULD BEHOOVE YOU TO CONCENTRATE.
I-IT'S NOT LIKE I MEANT TO FALL ASLEEP.
MMNH.
I WAS UP EXCEPTIONALLY EARLY THIS MORNING...
I HAVE AN ILLNESS THAT MAKES MY EYELIDS HEAVY WHENEVER I LOOK AT CALCULATIONS...
ふにゃー
DOOOZE
THERE IS NO SUCH ILLNESS.
WH-WHAT I MEAN TO SAY IS, ERM...
?

IF I MAY GUESS...DID YOU NOT GET SUFFICIENT REST?
JOLT
DID YOU NOT GO STRAIGHT TO BED AFTER WE WERE FOUND LAST NIGHT, DESPITE YOUR EXHAUSTION?
OR IS IT SOMETHING ELSE?
GH...
GUH...
SILENCE, YOU...
I WON'T TELL YOU...
NEVER...!
DEAREST BROTHER BRUNO SWORE ME TO SECRECY!
I'M NOT HIDING ANYTHING, ALL RIGHT!?
FWAP
YOU'RE CLEARLY HIDING SOME-THING.

NO, NO, NO! I WON'T TELL!
TRULY!?
YES, YES, I KNOW. I WON'T PRESS THE ISSUE...
GLOW
ぱあっ
SO SIMPLE...

PURSUING THE MATTER WILL ONLY INTERRUPT HIS LESSONS, SO I'LL LEAVE IT BE...
THAT CONCLUDES YOUR LESSONS FOR TODAY, PRINCE LEONHARD.
GOOD WORK.
F...FI-NALLY...
ぐったり
SLUMP
IF YOU'LL EXCUSE ME.
SHUT
DEAREST BROTHER BRUNO...
...SWORE ME TO SECRECY!
....
I CAN'T HELP BUT WONDER.

I'LL QUESTION THE OTHER THREE...
...DURING THEIR LESSONS.
BRUNO'S ROOM
I-I SAID NOTHING AT ALL TO LEONHARD!
LET US BEGIN THE LESSON, MASTER!
YOUR HIGHNESS, YOUR BOOK IS UPSIDE DOWN.
LICHT'S ROOM
BRUNIE AND LEONIE'S LITTLE SECRET? SURE, I'LL TELL YOU...
...IF YOU MAKE TODAY'S LESSON ONE ABOUT WAYS TO NURTURE LOVE WITH THE OPPOSITE SEX. ♡
NO.
KAI'S ROOM
AHEM... PRINCE KAI.
PRINCE.
PRINCE ...?
ふに PET
ふに PET
ふに PET
ふに PET
ふに PET
ふに PET
ふに PET
ふに PET
ふに PET
ふに PET

KAW!
KAW!
THERE.
LESSONS ARE DONE FOR THE DAY, AND I'VE WRITTEN MY REPORT TO THE KING.

WHILE I COULDN'T TELL IF PRINCE KAI IS INVOLVED...
PET
ふに...
...IT SEEMS CERTAIN THAT THE PRINCES ARE HIDING SOMETHING FROM ME.
POMF
ぽん

THE PRINCES INTEND TO PLAY A PRANK ON ME, DO THEY?
THE ROYAL TUTOR LETS OUT A SIGH AT HOW EASILY HE WAS ABLE TO SEE THROUGH THIS SCHEME.
TSK!

THEY MAY BE PRINCES, BUT THEY ARE STILL CHILDREN, AND BOYS WILL BE BOYS.
EEP!
...OR PUTTING SOMETHING DOWN THE BACK OF MY COLLAR...
MAKING SOMETHING FALL ON ME...
OW!
HMM. I'LL MAKE A NOTE OF THIS.
GURGLE
HMM. WHERE IS MY DINNER?
I DO BELIEVE IT IS TO BE DELIVERED TO MY ROOM.
KNOCK KNOCK
AHA. SPEAK OF THE DEVIL.
DINNER, DINNER...
KACHAK
FIDGET FIDGET
U-UM, HEINE...
W-WOULD YOU...JOIN ME FOR A STROLL...?
OH, IT'S ONLY YOU, PRINCE LEON-HARD?
PULLLLLL
WHAT DO YOU MEAN, "ONLY ME"!?
DON'T CLOSE THE DOOR IN MY FACE, YOU HEARTLESS TEACHER!

LOOK, I'M GOING OUT OF MY WAY TO INVITE YOU ON A WALK.
YOU SHOULD BE HONORED!
COME ALONG, THEN!
AS YOU WISH.
GOOD HEAVENS. PRINCE LEONHARD ASKING ME TO ACCOMPANY HIM?
A SUSPICIOUS ACT FROM THE VERY START.

HE'S LEADING ME TO A TRAP HOLE OR SOME SIMILAR PRANK, ISN'T HE?
AS AN ADULT, PERHAPS I SHOULD HUMOR HIM BY PURPOSEFULLY FALLING FOR HIS TRAP...

HMM...?

...PRINCE? THIS IS NOT SO MUCH A STROLL ...
...AS IT IS YOU CLEARLY MOVING ME SOME-WHERE.
...GH!
FLAIL
FLAIL
LOOK, JUST WAIT HERE A MOMENT.
LICHT! CAN I OPEN THE DOOR YET?
WHISPER
NOOO! WE STILL NEED A LITTLE TIME...

WHAT !!?
I ALREADY HAVE HIM HERE!
BAM
BUT THOSE TWO ARE...
AHHH, BRUNIE! KAINIE! HURRY, HURRY!
THEY'RE SQUABBLING OVER SOME-THING.
HOW TEDIOUS...

YOUR HIGHNESS? YOU NEEDN'T STRAIN YOURSELF HIDING THIS SURPRISE OF YOURS.
I HIGHLY DOUBT WHAT-EVER YOU'VE CONCOCTED CAN SURPRISE ME, IN ANY CASE...
KREEEAK

WELCOME ...
...TO WEISBURG PALACE!

... THIS IS...
YOUR WELCOMING PARTY.
IT WAS MY IDEA. IT'S BUT A MODEST PARTY, BUT WE ALL HAD A HAND IN PREPARING IT.
HMPH.
KAI GATHERED THE FLOWERS AND FRUIT FOR THE CENTER-PIECES.
...WENT TO THE GARDENS ...
... AFTER LESSONS ...
LICHT ARRANGED THE TABLE.
I WAS CONSULTING WITH A PROFESSIONAL BEFORE YOU CAME ALONG.
A LADY I KNOW WHO WORKS AT A FAMOUS RESTAU-RANT.
SWOON SWOON
YOU SHOULD ARRANGE IT LIKE THIS...

AND LEONHARD WENT HUNTING TO PROVIDE THE MEAT.
GLANCE
......

...WHAT WAS THAT ABOUT NOT BEING SURPRISED, HMM?
YOU'VE BEEN STRUCK DUMB!
MY...
I REALIZED YOUR HIGHNESSES WERE HIDING SOMETHING.
BUT I WAS CONVINCED IT WAS SOME KIND OF MISCHIEF.
CONSIDERING IT WAS A SURPRISE, YOU WERE HALF-RIGHT!
HOW COULD YOU THINK SUCH A THING, MASTER!?
BOLT

IF EVER YOU ARE THREATENED BY SUCH WICKEDNESS, MASTER, I WILL STOP IT AT ANY COST!
I WOULD GIVE MY VERY LIFE FOR YOURS ...!
PLEASE DON'T.
YOU ARE A PRINCE.
CLENCH

PRINCE LEON-HARD...
...YOU SACRIFICED SLEEP FOR MY SAKE?
MASTERRR...
ALTHOUGH, I STILL CANNOT APPROVE OF SLEEPING DURING LESSONS.
I-IT'S NOT LIKE I DID IT FOR YOU...!
I WANTED TO HELP DEAREST BROTHER BRUNO, THAT'S ALL.
I WOULDN'T HAVE BOTH-ERED RIDING OUT TO THE MOUNTAINS FIRST THING IN THE MORNING OTHERWISE.
BUT... HEH...
I DID ENJOY PULLING ONE OVER ON A TEACHER...
SNEER
MY CLEVER MISDIRECTION LEFT YOU COMPLETELY UNAWARE OF OUR SURPRISE!
WHAT SAY YOU!? HOW DOES IT FEEL TO BE FOOLED BY YOUR OWN STUDENT!?
HA HA
HA HA HA HA HA!
I WAS NOT. YOU WERE THE MOST OBVIOUSLY SUSPICIOUS.

THE QUEEN MOTHER HERSELF JOINS US? I AM HONORED.
WHAT!?
MY, MY. WHO MIGHT THIS YOUNG LADY BE?
HEE HEE. MY GRANDSONS INVITED ME.
THIS IS MY YOUNGEST GRANDCHILD.
HELLO. I'M ADELE!
OH, THE PRINCESS...
IT IS AN HONOR TO MAKE YOUR ACQUAINTANCE, PRINCESS ADELE.
I AM HEINE, THE ROYAL TUTOR.
SHE IS STILL QUITE YOUNG.
EH HEH! HEH!
I WOULD NOT BE SURPRISED TO LEARN SHE IS YOUNG ENOUGH TO BE MY DAUGHTER.
D'AWW, YOU TWO MAKE THE CUTEST COUPLE!
WHOO-HOOO!
CONGRATS, KIDS!
SHOCK

WATCH YOUR TONGUE, LICHT!
POUT
I AM A GROWN ADULT.
AH-HA-HA! IT WAS JUST A JOKE!
A TASTE-LESS JOKE.
ADELE IS BUT THREE YEARS OF AGE.

TO PROPOSE THAT A GIRL SO INEXPERI-ENCED IS FIT TO BE MASTER'S WIFE...IS POSITIVELY ABSURD...!!
GRIT
THAT'S WHAT BOTHERS YOU?
WHY ARE YOU ACTING LIKE AN IN-LAW?

HEINE, YOU INSOLENT LITTLE IMP...! HOW DARE YOU HAVE DEAREST BROTHER BRUNO'S ATTENTION ...!
RRRUMBLE
SUCH BOTHER-SOME BROTHERS.

LISTEN, ADELE, THAT TEACHER MAY BE SMALL, BUT HE'S A DEVIL!
STAY FAR, FAR AWAY FROM HIM!
DEH-VULL?
MUST YOU INSULT ME?
WHAT A DREAD-FUL THING TO SAY!
RATTLE
RATTLE

...FOOD'S HERE...
...EAT TOGETHER... FRIENDS...
LOOM
JUMP
Y-YES, ELDER BROTHER...

WHERE'S... TEACHER'S SEAT...?
FWIP
MASTER WILL SIT AT THE HEAD OF THE TABLE, OF COURSE!
WANDER
WANDER
EVERYONE ELSE IS SEATED ACCORDING TO THEIR RANK!
FWIP
WHOA, BRUNIE'S PULLING OUT ALL THE STOPS.
DOES IT MATTER WHERE WE SIT?
YOU THOUGHT OF EVERY-THING! THAT'S MY DEAREST BROTHER BRUNO...!

PERFECTION
きっちり
KLATTER
ガラ
RATTLE
ガラ
WE, THE STAFF OF THE ROYAL KITCHEN...
...WOULD LIKE TO WELCOME HERR WITTGENSTEIN WITH OUR FINEST DISHES.
GLEAM
パッ
OOH!

CLINK
WOULD YOU PREFER WINE OR BEER?
NEITHER, THANK YOU. MAY I HAVE WATER, THE SAME AS EVERYONE ELSE?
AHEM.
WELL, AS I WAS THE ONE TO PLAN THIS PARTY...
...I SHALL LEAD US OFF WITH A TOAST.
PROST!

PROST!
CLINK
NOW, ENJOY YOUR DINNER.
PROST!
CLINK

MMMM! GOOD STUFF!
FIDGET
FIDGET

IS SOME-THING THE MATTER, PRINCE LEON-HARD?
N-NO! I WAS JUST WONDERING HOW THE VENISON FROM THE DEER I SHOT TURNED OUT...
IT LOOKS DIVINE! YOU'RE AMAZING, LEONIE!
WOW! INCREDIBLE!
I WOULD EXPECT NOTHING LESS.
SQUIRM
SQUIRM
HE CLEARLY WANTS TO BE PRAISED.
FIDGET
FIDGET
FIDGET

MAY I PRESENT THE MAIN DISH.
JOLT
JUMP
HERE IT IS! IT'S MY TIME TO—

CHARRED

...I'M SORRY, LEON-HARD.
I CAN EXPLAIN...

AFTER YOU FELLED THAT DEER YOURSELF...
...WE WANTED TO COOK THE MEAT OUR-SELVES AS WELL.
I THOUGHT IT WOULD BE MOST APPROPRIATE TO PRESENT A DISH THAT WE BROTHERS HAD CREATED ENTIRELY BY OURSELVES TO MASTER...
WE COOKED IT WHEN YOU WENT TO SUMMON MASTER...
BUT YOU SEE THE RESULT ...
BRUNIE GOT DIS-TRACTED.
PSST!
NO! I ASKED YOU TO KEEP AN EYE ON IT THEN!
WHAAAT? WAY TO PASS THE BLAME, JERK!
LEON-HARD...
FREEZE
BLOOOSH
S-SORRY! I'M REAL SORRY, LEONIE!
PANIC
PANIC
PANIC
I-I'M SINCERELY SORRY...

B-BUT THERE'S ONE SERVING'S WORTH THAT ISN'T BURNT!
POP
TEACH, YOU'RE THE GUEST OF HONOR...
...SO WE'LL SERVE IT TO YOU!
CLINK
NH... NGH...
......
CLINK
...YES...
IT TASTES EXQUI-SITE.

THANK YOU, PRINCE LEONHARD.

SIR, IF I MAY IMPOSE UPON YOU...
...WOULD YOU PLEASE CUT THIS STEAK INTO ENOUGH PORTIONS THAT EVERY-ONE MAY PARTAKE?
TH-THERE'S NO NEED FOR THAT! WE WANTED YOU TO EAT IT!
THE DISH WAS GIVEN TO ME.
THERE-FORE, I AM FREE TO SHARE IT WITH WHOM-EVER I PLEASE.
AM I MISTAKEN?
...!
......
A SOUND ARGU-MENT.

BITE-SIZED
WAAH! IT'S CUTE!
MINI-STEAK!!
OH! EVEN THESE SMALL PIECES ARE FULL OF FLAVOR. DELICIOUS!
NOD NOD
HEH! PRETTY GOOD! ♪
ALL THANKS TO MY EXQUISITE SEASONING!!
IT'S ALL THANKS TO LEONHARD FOR BRINGING IN THE DEER, YOU MEAN!
YOU'RE TOO QUICK TO PRAISE YOURSELF!
OW!
ISN'T THAT NICE, PRINCE LEONHARD? EVERYONE WAS PLEASED WITH IT.
YOU SEE? NO HARD WORK GOES UNREWARDED.
WH-WHAT!?

NH...!
DON'T FORGET— I AM NOT HAPPY TO HAVE A TEACHER HERE!!
I STILL WANT TO BE RID OF YOU, UNDER-STAND!?
LEONIE'S SO SHYYY!
YES, YES, I KNOW.
I COULD NOT BE MORE SERI-OUS!!

I FELT SO RESTLESS IN THIS ROOM LAST NIGHT, BUT THAT FEELING HAS SUBSIDED SOMEWHAT...
I BELIEVE I WILL SLEEP WELL TONIGHT.

I'M SURE IT'S BECAUSE THE PRINCES GAVE ME A SIGN THAT IT'S ALL RIGHT FOR ME TO BE HERE.
A WELCOME PARTY FOR ME?
I COULDN'T BE MORE PLEASED.

—BUT THE TRUTH IS...

...I DON'T BELONG HERE...

• The Royal Tutor 1 End •

THE ROYAL TUTOR

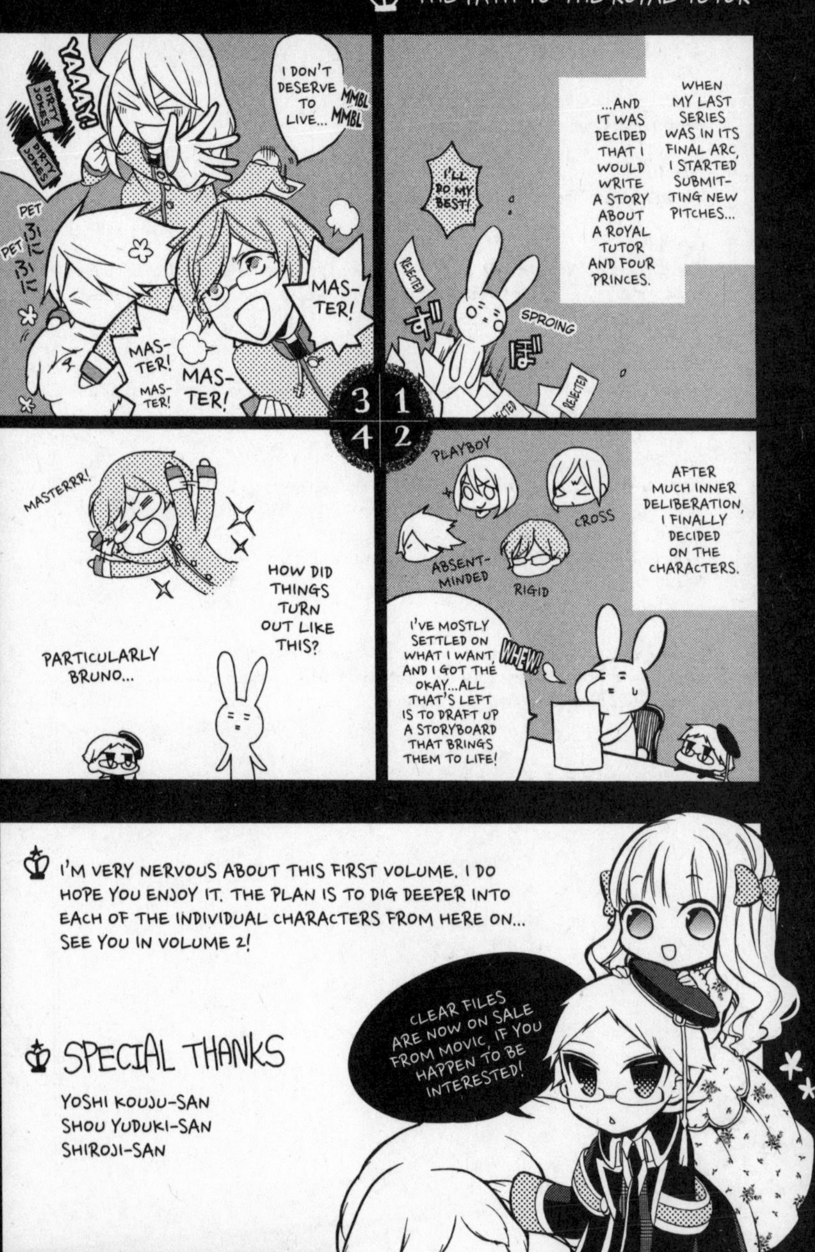
THE PATH TO THE ROYAL TUTOR
WHEN MY LAST SERIES WAS IN ITS FINAL ARC, I STARTED SUBMITTING NEW PITCHES...
...AND IT WAS DECIDED THAT I WOULD WRITE A STORY ABOUT A ROYAL TUTOR AND FOUR PRINCES.
I'LL DO MY BEST!
REJECTED
SPROING
REJECTED
AFTER MUCH INNER DELIBERATION, I FINALLY DECIDED ON THE CHARACTERS.
PLAYBOY
CROSS
ABSENT-MINDED
RIGID
I'VE MOSTLY SETTLED ON WHAT I WANT, AND I GOT THE OKAY...ALL THAT'S LEFT IS TO DRAFT UP A STORYBOARD THAT BRINGS THEM TO LIFE!
WHEW!
I DON'T DESERVE TO LIVE...
MMBL MMBL
YAAAY!
DIRTY JOKES
DIRTY JOKES
PET
PET
ふにふに
MAS-TER!
MAS-TER!
MAS-TER!
MAS-TER!
MASTERRR!
HOW DID THINGS TURN OUT LIKE THIS?
PARTICULARLY BRUNO...
I'M VERY NERVOUS ABOUT THIS FIRST VOLUME. I DO HOPE YOU ENJOY IT. THE PLAN IS TO DIG DEEPER INTO EACH OF THE INDIVIDUAL CHARACTERS FROM HERE ON... SEE YOU IN VOLUME 2!
SPECIAL THANKS
YOSHI KOUJU-SAN
SHOU YUDUKI-SAN
SHIROJI-SAN
CLEAR FILES ARE NOW ON SALE FROM MOVIC, IF YOU HAPPEN TO BE INTERESTED!

Translation Notes

Page 3
***Freut mich*:** German for "nice to meet you."

Page 10
Queen mother: The mother of the reigning king.

Page 48
***Torte*:** A kind of rich, multilayered cake. Prince Leonhard is specifically imagining Sacher torte, a Viennese specialty consisting of chocolate cake with layers separated by apricot jam.

Page 55
***Melange*:** German for "blend." A specialty coffee drink similar to a cappuccino, and a popular beverage in Vienna.

Page 76
***Ringstrasse*:** German for "ring road," the real-world Ringstrasse is a boulevard circling the city center of Vienna, Austria. The Ringstrasse project began as a replacement for the inner city walls, which were demolished by decree of Emperor Franz Joseph I in 1857, and the road's construction coincided with a liberal social shift away from class elitism.

Page 77
Public operettas: In modern times, we might consider the opera to be high culture, but it was popular entertainment for all social classes in 1890s Austria-Hungary, the basis for *The Royal Tutor*'s Kingdom of Granzreich.

Page 131
Grading in Japan: In Japan where the manga was penned, incorrect answers are typically marked with checkmarks, and correct answers are marked with circles.

The Royal Tutor ❶

Higasa Akai

Translation: Amanda Haley • Lettering: Abigail Blackman

Yen Press
1290 Avenue of the Americas
New York, NY 10104

Visit us at yenpress.com
facebook.com/yenpress
twitter.com/yenpress
yenpress.tumblr.com
instagram.com/yenpress

First Yen Press Print Edition: May 2017
Originally published as an eBook in August 2015 by Yen Press.

Yen Press is an imprint of Yen Press, LLC.
The Yen Press name and logo are trademarks of Yen Press, LLC.

The publisher is not responsible for websites (or their content) that are not owned by the publisher.

Library of Congress Control Number: 2017938422

ISBN: 978-0-316-43979-4 (paperback)

10 9 8 7 6 5 4 3

WOR

Printed in the United States of America